Private Spaces in Public Places

PRIVATE SPACES
IN PUBLIC PLACES

Laura Walikainen Rouleau

Johns Hopkins University Press
Baltimore

© 2024 Johns Hopkins University Press
All rights reserved. Published 2024
Printed in the United States of America on acid-free paper
2 4 6 8 9 7 5 3 1

Johns Hopkins University Press
2715 North Charles Street
Baltimore, Maryland 21218
www.press.jhu.edu

Library of Congress Cataloging-in-Publication Data

Names: Rouleau, Laura W., 1982– author.
Title: Private spaces in public places / Laura W. Rouleau.
Description: Baltimore : Johns Hopkins University Press, 2024. | Outgrowth of the author's thesis (doctoral)—University of Delaware, 2014, under the title: Private spaces in public places : exploring the boundary of privacy, 1880–1930. | Includes bibliographical references and index.
Identifiers: LCCN 2023059551 | ISBN 9781421449999 (hardcover) | ISBN 9781421450001 (ebook)
Subjects: LCSH: Public spaces—Social aspects—United States—History—19th century. | Public spaces—Social aspects—United States—History—20th century. | Privacy—United States—History—19th century. | Privacy—United States—History—20th century. | Architecture and society—History—19th century. | Architecture and society—History—20th century.
Classification: LCC HT185 .R66 2024 | DDC 712—dc23/eng/20240222
LC record available at https://lccn.loc.gov/2023059551

A catalog record for this book is available from the British Library.

Special discounts are available for bulk purchases of this book. For more information, please contact Special Sales at specialsales@jh.edu.

CONTENTS

Acknowledgments vii

1
Privacy in Public: *How Did We Get Here?* 1

2
Department Store Fitting Rooms: *A Gendered Privacy* 9

3
Public Baths: *Cleansing the "Classed" Body* 36

4
Creating Privacy in Public: *Public Comfort Stations* 63

5
Learning Privacy: *Public School Locker Rooms* 89

Conclusion 112

Notes 115
Index 133

ACKNOWLEDGMENTS

Many teachers, colleagues, friends and family members have accompanied me on my scholarly journey through historical fitting rooms, restrooms, baths and locker rooms. I am extremely grateful to my dissertation adviser, Dr. Arwen Mohun, for her insights and advice throughout this venture, from her encouragement in our initial discussions to her patient reading of many, many subsequent drafts. During her engaging class on the history of Victorian America, Dr. Katherine Grier sparked my initial interest in this era. Dr. Susan Strasser taught me about practicing the craft of history, and it was during one of her courses that I began to think about private spaces in public. Dr. Barbara Penner's scholarship helped lay the groundwork for this research. Professor Kim Hoagland's study of Copper Country spaces informs this work and continues to inspire me. Well before graduate school, Professor Hoagland and Professor Larry Lankton introduced me to the field of material culture studies and fostered my interest in the history of my own community. I am thankful to all of them for their mentorship, guidance, thoughts, and insights.

In more recent years, I've had the opportunity to design and teach a course on the history of privacy at Michigan Technological University. The undergraduates in this class have challenged my assumptions and offered fresh perspectives on a subject I've been pondering for the past fifteen years. My colleagues in the Social Sciences Department have attentively read and listened to various iterations of this project, offering valuable suggestions throughout.

I am also indebted to the many supportive archivists and librarians at the Chicago History Museum, Hagley Museum and Library, Historical Society of Pennsylvania, Keweenaw National Historical Park, Michigan Technological University Archives and Copper Country Historical Collections, New

York Historical Society, New York Public Library, New York Transit Museum, University of Delaware Library, and Winterthur Museum and Library. This research was funded at critical junctures by the Society of Winterthur Fellows, Michigan Technological University, University of Delaware, Center for Material Culture Studies, and National Endowment for the Humanities. Early versions of several chapters benefited from the insights of participants at the Berkshire Conference on the History of Women, American Historical Association Annual Meeting, American Studies Association Annual Meeting, Material Culture Symposium for Emerging Scholars at Delaware, Parsons/Cooper-Hewitt Symposium on the Decorative Arts and Design, Producing Publics: Architecture, Agency and Social Space Symposium at Cornell University, and Washington University's Graduate Conference on the History of the Body.

I am grateful for this opportunity to publicly thank those whose contributions to this endeavor might have otherwise remained hidden from view. This book is also the work of my family, whose love, understanding, and encouragement are behind every word I wrote. My brother, John, continually asked, "How's the book going?" and my quest to give him a good answer kept me going, as did his humor. My parents constantly encouraged me to do what I loved, from when I was a five-year-old who wanted to be "a ballerina and a waitress," to when I declared I was moving to Delaware to study material culture and history. The older I get, the more I realize how precious and rare such support really is. My mother believed in and encouraged me from the very beginning of this and all of my projects. My father has been my patient editor, thoughtfully reading everything I have ever written since kindergarten; I have always emulated him as a writer and scholar.

To my husband, Mark: your constant faith in me has sustained me throughout this and our many other voyages together. Thank you for listening, responding, encouraging, and commiserating on this spatial journey. Much of what follows was hashed out over our long walks in the woods with our dogs, Louis and Sophie. In those woods, as in our lives, you've always challenged us to take the path "less traveled by, and that has made all the difference."

Finally, I dedicate this book to my children, Ann and Henri, who gave me the greatest motivation to write, as well as new insights into "bodies in public." Thank you for helping me see these spaces anew, through your eyes. And thank you for insisting, from a very early age, "Mom, I need privacy."

CHAPTER ONE

Privacy in Public

How Did We Get Here?

As I was working on this study of the history of privacy, arguments surrounding privacy's very meaning were exploding into our collective consciousness over the issue of restroom access. Back in March 2016, North Carolina was the first state to pass a law requiring all "bathrooms or changing facilities" located in public schools and public agencies to "be designated for and used only by persons based on their biological sex [as stated on a person's birth certificate]."[1] Then Iowa, Idaho, and Arkansas passed similar laws in 2023.[2] Also in 2023, Florida passed a "Safety in Private Spaces Act," mandating that "females and males should be provided restrooms and changing facilities for their exclusive use, respective to their sex, in order to maintain public safety, decency, decorum, and privacy," defining a person's sex "as indicated by the person's sex chromosomes, naturally occurring sex hormones, and internal and external genitalia present at birth."[3] The following year, Utah passed a bill that defined "a restroom or changing room within a publicly owned or controlled facility, where an individual has a reasonable expectation of privacy" as a "privacy space."[4] This law prohibited individuals from entering a "sex-designated privacy space" that did not correspond to their sex assigned at birth.[5] These laws stood in stark contrast to a 2013 California law that stated that a public school student "shall be permitted to . . . use facilities consistent with his or her gender identity, irrespective of the gender listed on the pupil's records."[6] California lawmakers proposed a 2023 update to this law that would require all-gender restrooms in schools throughout the state by 2026.[7] An intense public debate ensued after each law was passed, in which various parties argued about issues concerning gender, safety, and identity. The debate itself took on a highly gendered tone as the majority of concerns over these bills had to do with anxiety over the appearance of "males" in "female" facilities; almost no mention was made of concern about the opposite scenario. And politicians on both sides of the debate couched their arguments in terms of "protecting privacy."[8]

While this debate played out in popular discourse, I had the opportunity to view the space of the public restroom through a new set of eyes: those of my recently potty-trained two-year-old daughter. Almost unconsciously and without any discussion with my husband, I took on the responsibility of taking my daughter into women's restrooms. (On later reflection, I came to understand that my husband and I had been socialized into accepting certain gender roles without question.) As my daughter encountered public restrooms for the first time, these sites became strange to me all over again. I was reminded of how loud, intimidating, and often unpleasant these spaces are. I was reacquainted with the socialization process necessary to persuade children to relieve themselves in public, in the presence of strangers. My daughter was, quite naturally, uncomfortable in these spaces. And I found myself asking, How did we get here? How did the act of relieving ourselves in public ever become acceptable?

The answer: Our society has been able to construct a socially acceptable level of privacy within these public spaces. This privacy is predicated on exclusion: exclusion in a spatial sense, through visual barriers, as well as social exclusion founded on gender segregation. For the most part, society appears to have accepted this definition of privacy in order to perform this private, bodily function in a public place. My family is just one example of this socialization and acceptance in practice. But when this sense of privacy appears to be threatened, as highlighted by the responses to the recent restroom laws, the very meaning of privacy is called into question.

At the core of these contemporary restroom experiences have been questions of perpetual concern to our postindustrial society: What is privacy? How is privacy defined and experienced? Who gets to define it, and why? How does this definition change over time? And how does this definition impact people's lives? This book presents a historical moment in the early modern era when the meaning of privacy was also in flux. By interrogating how privacy has been negotiated in the past, we can begin to understand the historical foundations for our current understanding and expectations surrounding the concept of privacy.

Privacy is a socially contested concept. At the turn of the twentieth century, several new spaces were developing (including public restrooms) that brought the question of privacy into public discourse. Much as in our current debates over the meaning of privacy, social commentators at the turn of the twentieth century largely framed their arguments through a highly gendered lens. Implicit in both modern and historical discussions surrounding gender and privacy is a preoccupation with the protection, through both differentiation and seclusion, of the female body. This protection could take on a spatial form, through physical barriers such as stall doors, or a social dimension, through the segregation of men and women. Both past and present discussions of privacy reveal anxiety over the physical and social protection of bodies, especially female bodies, while performing the private act of relieving themselves. This anxiety is heightened when privacy needs to be defined at sites that are otherwise public.

This book offers a working definition of privacy at the turn of the twentieth century: privacy was a spatial and social means of *exclusion*, based on the constructed categories of gender, race, class, and, at times, age. This definition captures how middle-class reformers, municipal officials, designers, and so on determined the appropriate division between public and private as new public institutions emerged that brought private acts into significantly more public places. This definition was physically manifested in the private spaces in public places that form the basis for my research. Examining the concept of privacy in this context has implications for the broader histories of sanitation, hygiene, public health, and public education at the turn of the twentieth century.

Today, we take the provision of private spaces in public places for granted, but during the late nineteenth and early twentieth centuries, such spaces were only beginning to be viewed as normal and necessary in US towns and cities. From approximately 1880 to 1930, a series of new sites—including department store fitting rooms, public baths, public restrooms, and public school locker rooms—were created to enable people to perform private activities, such as bathing and undressing, in public. Returning to the origins of these now-ubiquitous sites allows us to view these spaces as strange again, questioning their very form and design.

In public restrooms, department store fitting rooms, locker rooms, and public baths, privacy was constructed both physically and socially. Visual and, at times, aural barriers established physical privacy in public. But, for middle-class creators, gender and racial segregation, as well as social class distinction, were just as essential to creating this privacy so that intimate, bodily activities could be acceptably performed in public. Although the sites' designers and creators sought to impose their middle-class understanding of privacy, actual users were often members of the working class. The self-conscious construction and regulation of the emerging sites offer insights into the historical definition of privacy during this time.[9]

Sites such as public restrooms, fitting rooms, public baths, and locker rooms were created because they solved problems. The human body has certain biological needs. In American society, it is not ordinarily acceptable to perform all of these needs outside of one's home. These taboo tasks include the removal of waste, cleansing the body, and dressing and undressing. Restrooms allow for the removal of waste; public baths and locker rooms provide space to cleanse the body; and fitting rooms allow for dressing and undressing.

Beyond the physical, these sites solved social problems as well. These spaces became more common and more necessary as social forces, including industrialization and urbanization, increasingly drew people out of their private homes and into public places. People spending long hours in department stores, on public transportation, and in schools required spaces to cleanse, relieve, and clothe their bodies. Middle-class women who frequented developing department stores needed fitting rooms where they could try on clothing that was now ready-made.[10] The growing number of working-class people required the use of public bathing facilities, because their housing usually offered none.[11] Men and women from across social classes needed public toilets as they spent more time away from home.[12] And by the early twentieth century, public school children were inculcated into performing such private activities in public in their school locker rooms.[13]

This book is a spatial journey. I analyze four case studies centered on distinct bodily activities performed in emerging private spaces at the turn of the twentieth century in order to discover how privacy was physically and socially constructed within these spaces. I chose fitting rooms, public baths, locker rooms, and restrooms because they center on some of the most essential human bodily activities, including relieving oneself, bathing, and dressing and undressing. These activities are considered highly private by most people in the United States, so I needed to understand how they came to be acceptably performed in public. These specialized private spaces within public spaces were consciously created to provide privacy to their users, and hence facilitated the activities discussed here.

I also chose these spaces as case studies because they all emerged during the same era, from approximately 1880 to 1930. I was intrigued that an era that was widely known for its preoccupation with modesty and decorum would have produced dedicated spaces where people could bathe, dress, undress, and relieve themselves in public. But the discussions surrounding the development of spaces were firmly planted in the Progressivism and consumerism that were also hallmarks of this age.

These sites were also selected because they demonstrate different aspects of the process of defining privacy. Department store fitting rooms developed so that middle-class women would have access to privacy in the newly emerging department store. The interclass contact between customers and saleswomen illustrates that the essential importance of gender segregation outweighed, at times, class distinctions. The discussion on public baths uncovers the process through which social reformers, municipal officials, and designers imposed their middle-class definition of privacy on the working-class bath patrons. The analysis of public restrooms allows us to explore how gender, race, and class exclusion made it socially acceptable for people to relieve themselves in public. The study of early public restrooms also offers insight into how people actually used these sites and how user activities were often at odds with the designers' intentions. Studying the emergence of public school locker rooms reveals the socialization process involved in training adolescents to perform the private act of cleansing their bodies in public.

The following chapters build on one another by exploring the various ways privacy was contested, even as members of the middle class were working to create privacy in newly emerging private spaces in public. The first chapter focuses on department store fitting rooms to offer an origin story, as fitting rooms were some of the earliest examples of these sites. As department store owners and designers created fitting rooms for their middle-class female customers, they needed to convince women that these new sites afforded privacy similar to what they experienced within the domestic sphere. Here, the contestation over privacy was whether or not it could exist in public spaces. The second spatial case study views the public bath movement through the class conflict embodied by the middle-class creators and the working-class users of these sites. Public restrooms inform the third case study. These sites in particular allow us to begin to understand users' experience of privacy. Through their performance of alternative or prohibited activities within these sites, we can uncover an unexpected dialogue between users and creators. With public restrooms, we can also begin to view social exclusion explicitly based on gender, class, and race. The final spatial case study focuses on public school locker rooms. Public school students at the turn of the twentieth century were often members of the working class as well as immigrants or the children of immigrants and were much younger than the authority figures they encountered. These students' subordinate status facilitated their socialization into a specific, middle-class definition of privacy.

All of these sites offered privacy based on spatial and social exclusion. But it is important to recognize who was being excluded and who was in control of this exclusion. These spaces were all designed, created, implemented, and regulated by members of the middle to upper classes. Therefore, this exclusion was based on largely middle-class norms of gender, class, race, and even age segregation. This foundation translated into an uneven experience of bodily privacy, as women often experienced a higher level of privacy than men, persons of color were often not guaranteed the same access to privacy as white users, and greater levels of privacy could often be had for those who could afford it.

But historical bodies don't always behave. As my research shows, these spaces were also contested. The very privacy these sites afforded also created an opportunity to transgress the intentions of their middle-class creators. Saleswomen were reprimanded for lounging in customers' fitting rooms.[14] Police officers patrolled public baths to prevent petty crimes, including theft.[15] Public school students, under almost constant surveillance, appear to have been less successful in their attempts to transgress the rules of the locker room.[16] And public restrooms provided space for illicit sexual encounters.[17] These transgressions often led to a redesign of the space or increased presence of attendants, managers, or police.

Taken together, the case studies allow for a critical exploration of the key variables of social exclusion: gender, class, race, and age. In all of the case studies, gender segregation emerges as the most fundamental element to this definition of privacy. The case of the department store fitting room allows us to explore the interplay of gender and class. Here we see that interclass contact was acceptable as long as these spaces were gender segregated. Public baths were created for the working class, allowing the middle class to self-exclude and bathe at home in newly created, dedicated bathrooms. But gender separation was strictly enforced. In the public restroom, we find the interplay of gender, race, and class. Restrooms always separated men and women, but I have located evidence of explicit racial segregation during this era of initial implementation only in certain geographic locations. Class exclusion was of secondary or tertiary importance. Within public school locker rooms, students learned the primary importance of gender while learning to bathe at school. Through constant monitoring, students also learned that access to complete privacy was often age-dependent.

The emergence of these spaces is embedded in several concurrent social transformations. The forces of industrialization, immigration, and urbanization altered the public and private landscape of the United States, necessitating the creation of private spaces in public. The rise of consumerism and consumption at the turn of the twentieth century is embodied in the development of the department store fitting room. The Progressive movement's focus on public health, hygiene, sanitation, and education is reflected in the creation of public restrooms, baths, and school locker rooms.

The social contestation of privacy transpired throughout the country at the turn of the twentieth century. The locations of the emerging private spaces in public places investigated here offer insight into how pervasive this definition of privacy was during this time. From urbanizing New York to industrializing northern Michigan, people were increasingly performing private bodily activities away from home. The similarities of the physical appearance of these sites across geographical locations demonstrate the pervasiveness of the social norms underlying the creation of these spaces.

Although privacy is often discussed in public discourse and scholarship, the term is rarely defined. My work problematizes privacy in an effort to understand its historical context and how it evolved. I build on the work of other scholars who have conceptualized privacy in several historical contexts.[18] Scholars of women's history established the gendered dimension of privacy, as well as a public/domestic dichotomy that reflected the ideology of separate spheres.[19] Studies of hotels, railroad cars, and restrooms have advanced these domestic and gendered interpretations of privacy.[20] Other scholars have revealed how access to privacy defined identity and how, in turn, restriction of access also helped draw the line between public and private.[21] Still others have emphasized the physical and visual creation of the private in public spaces, including public restrooms.[22]

Throughout my research, I have drawn on a variety of sources and modes of analysis to connect the social and spatial construction of privacy throughout these sites. In each case study, I outline how people performed these activities before these new spaces were created to highlight the reasons for the emergence of these new sites. I analyzed the writings of contemporary social commentators and investigated available oral histories to uncover how people relieved themselves, bathed, and dressed and undressed prior to this change. I then shifted my focus to the initial development of these spaces and the discussions surrounding their design. Dialogues about what these spaces should look like, and why, played out in contemporary periodicals, prescriptive literature, and trade catalogs. I proceeded to a material-culture-based analysis utilizing floor plans, drawings, blueprints, and contemporary photographs, which allowed me to enter the spaces themselves and gain a sense for how they functioned. Finally, I searched for the human element that enlivened these historical sites. I conducted interviews with individuals who had used these spaces and uncovered contemporary discussions of the attendants, managers, and other workers who were tasked with regulating and maintaining these spaces. These sources, while wide-ranging, did present challenges and limitations. Most of the published materials discussed northern, urban, industrial examples. While many of these sources did not overtly mention issues of race (with the exception of public restrooms located in the South), it can be inferred that race was another category of exclusion that was considered central to the definition of privacy.

In the decades surrounding the turn of the twentieth century, these private spaces in public places became not only accepted but expected. And our continued acceptance of these spaces is revealed every time we undress, relieve, or cleanse our bodies in public.

CHAPTER TWO

Department Store Fitting Rooms

A Gendered Privacy

In *A Friendly Guide-Book to the Wanamaker Store*, a pamphlet published in 1915, advertisers promoted the women's clothing section of the department store as offering "seclusion from the usual shopping crowds . . . enabl[ing] women to select their purchases under the most ideal conditions of comfort, privacy, and artistic atmosphere."[1] As this pamphlet indicates, the privacy afforded to female, middle-class customers was of utmost concern to department store executives. But how did a grandiose public department store create privacy for its patrons?

In this chapter, I analyze the experience of privacy in our first spatial case study: department store fitting rooms. Early department store fitting rooms tended to have a similar layout and design. They were usually located along an exterior wall in a clothing department. Women and men always had separate fitting rooms. These spaces were almost always individual rooms, not common or group fitting rooms. Walls, doors, curtains, or a combination of these shielded users from outside view. Mirrors were provided in or near the fitting rooms. And the intended users of these sites were the white, middle-class women who frequented the department store.

Department store fitting rooms were physical spaces animated by bodily activities. This first spatial case study provides an important analysis, as these spaces were created to afford bodily privacy, which was deemed necessary because the acts of dressing and undressing were considered private. Department store fitting rooms are an early example of a private space in a public place that made it possible for people to achieve bodily privacy, which was essential for the private act of clothing one's body in a public setting.

By studying the fitting room, we can see how designers attempted to establish gender separation as an important component of privacy. The privacy expectations associated with dressing and undressing often emphasized gender separation as a way to achieve bodily privacy. Through the physical creation of these gender-separated spaces, middle-class designers socially constructed privacy at these sites to help achieve expectations about bodily privacy.

The department store fitting room also provides an essential basis of comparison for the case studies in later chapters of this book. This study sets the stage for the gender construction of each of the spaces that follow. And comparing fitting rooms to public baths, restrooms, and locker rooms allows us to consider how these spaces were socially constructed in different ways based on class.

The spatial case studies in this and the following chapters allow us to make observations not only about the origins of these sites but also about how these spaces embodied or encoded privacy expectations. To begin this analysis, we need to better understand how this version of bodily privacy, centered on dressing and undressing, was achieved prior to the existence of fitting rooms.

The acts of dressing and undressing prior to the existence of fitting rooms were typically done in the home for those who made their own clothing or in a dressmaker's shop for those who could afford to pay others to make their clothing. In these more traditional, often domestic settings, women could exclude any nonfamilial members of the public from intruding into their clothing experience. Dressing and undressing in those spaces enabled individuals to achieve bodily privacy by shutting themselves off from all others except the person helping them make the clothes (such as the seamstress or the dressmaker).

Private Clothing: Home Sewing or the Dressmaker's Shop

Prior to the emergence of department store fitting rooms, middle-class women achieved bodily privacy by dressing and undressing in their homes or dressmakers' shops while being fitted for custom-made clothing. Many of the middle-class women who flocked to early twentieth-century department stores had little or no experience with acquiring clothing in a public setting. During the early nineteenth century, men's, women's, and children's clothing was usually either custom-made at home by a friend or family member or by a professional tailor or dressmaker; the latter was cost-prohibitive for most working- and middle-class Americans.[2] Home sewing and the creation of the family's clothing were still considered a part of the household work for most

American women, especially working-class women, throughout most of the nineteenth century.³ Prior to the advent of mass-produced clothing, they had few alternatives for clothing their families besides home sewing. This process of making clothes was a personal, intimate one in which all parties involved were familiar with, if not related to, one another. And the actual manufacture of clothing usually took place within the private confines of the home. Thus the physical space of a private domestic setting, as well as the interpersonal relationships between friends and relatives, defined the intimate experience of women's clothing until the turn of the twentieth century.

Dressmakers either visited their customers in their homes or welcomed them to a shop space where women could dress and undress while maintaining bodily privacy. Even for middle- and upper-class women who could afford a dressmaker, their interaction with the dressmaker was personal and intimate. Although high-end dressmaking shops were large and elaborately decorated, most dressmakers invited patrons into their homes or "went out by the day" to visit patrons' homes to fit dresses.⁴ Many patrons experienced the clothes-purchasing process in the most private setting possible: their own homes. *Godey's Lady's Book* published a short story in 1854 about "Mrs. Murden's" first experience of having a dress made at an upscale professional dressmaker's shop. This story illustrates a typical clothing experience of a middle-class woman in the mid-nineteenth century. Mrs. Murden's usual, less expensive dressmaker, Miss Johns, came to Mrs. Murden's home and fit Mrs. Murden's dresses "in her own back parlor."⁵ Like Mrs. Murden, customers' experiences usually consisted of one-on-one encounters with the dressmaker who actually made the garment. These personal encounters between dressmakers and their customers created an intimate relationship that often developed over several years of patronage. Dressmakers often advertised via word of mouth, capitalizing on the close personal relationships they developed with their customers.⁶

The dressmaker's shop was a female-only space, allowing women to experience bodily privacy based on gender segregation. At this time, nearly all dressmakers and their assistants, if they had any, were women.⁷ This was certainly the experience of Mrs. Murden, who interacted with several female assistants in her first visit to a dressmaker's shop.⁸ In this way, the dressmakers and their female staff members mirrored the predominantly female circle of clothing creators found within the home. The personal interactions between the dressmaker, her female staff, and female patrons fostered an intimate relationship based on the custom-made dressmaking process. The exclusion of men from the spaces and experiences of clothing women's bodies served to underscore how privacy was defined and attained. This privacy was essential for women to perform the intimate activities of dressing and undressing.

Bodily privacy was viewed as necessary for these clothing experiences. Both of these processes—home sewing and professional dressmakers' work—produced custom-made clothing for the body of the woman who wore it. Fabric was cut out, pinned, and fitted directly onto the body of the eventual wearer, in what was known as the "pin-to-the-form" technique.[9] This involved pinning fabric to the corset or undergarments of the wearer, cutting the fabric to the correct size, and sewing the pieces together to create a finished, one-of-a-kind garment.[10] This experience was physically intimate for the customer, and it is understandable that a woman would allow only family members or a trusted local dressmaker to conduct this intimate activity with her.

Dressmakers, whether professional or not, had an intimate knowledge of the bodies of the women who would finally wear the garments. As a nineteenth-century British writer pointed out, "the dress-maker must be the perfect anatomist.... She must know how to hide all defects in the proportions of the body."[11] A dress was made for one woman specifically and would not fit anyone else without alteration. Thus, women's dresses of the early nineteenth century were the product of a personal relationship between the dressmaker and other women. In order for this level of intimacy to be achieved, women needed to be able to conduct this clothing process in private. This privacy was defined by familial relationship, in the case of home dressmaking, or a shared gender, in the case of professional dressmakers.

When the professional dressmaker owned a shop rather than conducting home visits, the shop usually contained a private room for fitting dresses to the customer. These rooms served as transitional spaces between the home and later department store fitting rooms. In the *Godey's* story, Mrs. Murden decided to go to a more expensive dressmaker to have a dress made from a "two dollar silk," the most expensive fabric Mrs. Murden had ever bought (women often purchased their own fabric and brought it to a dressmaker). During her first visit to a dressmaking shop, a shop assistant "asked Mrs. Murden into the inner apartment, with its curtains and lounges, its cheval glass [tall dressing mirror] reflecting the little woman's figure from head to foot."[12] These furnishings offered customers such as Mrs. Murden a comfortable space similar to the domestic environment experienced by home dressmakers. Mrs. Murden returned a week later to be "fitted." She was shown into the "fitting-room . . . quite a picture . . . [with] the lounges spread with dresses."[13] Inside the room, Mrs. Murden tried on the dress while the dressmaker "pulled and puckered, let out, and let in, the nicely fitting basque [type of dress]."[14] The interior, secluded location of the fitting room ensured visual and spatial privacy, as well as protection from outside viewers, for the dressmaker's customers. The interior also created an intimate setting in which customers could feel at ease during the physically intimate experience of custom-made dressmaking. These interiors referenced the domestic environment where outsiders and strangers could be excluded, aligning the dressmaker's shop with the domestic experience of privacy at home.

Although this story is indicative of the clothing experience for many nineteenth-century US women, most people living in the United States today do not wear custom-made clothing that was created specifically for our bodies by a relative or professional dressmaker or tailor. It is now the norm to try on mass-produced clothing in standardized sizes in a physical retail store. What happened? What changed between the traditional nineteenth-century clothing experience and today? Why did it become necessary to create the private space (the fitting room) in a public place (the department store) to achieve bodily privacy for those dressing and undressing in these spaces? The answer is that the rise of ready-made clothing, the growth of consumer culture, and the emergence of department stores precipitated the creation of fitting rooms as a private space designed in a public place for a specific intended user: white, middle-class women. With the growth of the department store and the development of ready-made clothing, women began to experience a shift in how they acquired new clothing at the turn of the twentieth century.

Public Clothing: Ready-Mades

Although department stores existed in American cities from the 1870s and 1880s, they did not begin to carry extensive ready-made clothing lines for women until the 1890s.[15] The introduction of the shirtwaist in the 1890s, along with similarly standardized clothing items, necessitated the creation of dressing rooms.[16] Ready-made clothing, department stores, and their fitting rooms eventually democratized the professional dressmaking experience. The advent of women's ready-made clothing in the late nineteenth century caused a shift away from custom-made dressmaking.

The first men's ready-made clothing factory was founded in 1831, and by the 1850s, the men's ready-made clothing industry had been well established.[17] But women had to wait until the 1890s for the widespread availability of ready-made dresses and suits (a set of clothing pieces such as a top and skirt that were designed to be worn together), although ready-made women's outer- and underwear appeared a bit earlier.[18] After the appearance and widespread acceptance of the jersey waist (a tight-fitting shirt "made of an elastic knitted material, conformed to the figure without the aid of a tailor") in the 1890s, the development of ready-made skirts and shirtwaists soon followed.[19] Shirtwaists were widely available in catalogs as well as clothing and department stores, where these "waists" were advertised as ready for "immediate wear."[20] By 1910, every item in a woman's wardrobe was available ready-made.[21] One department store periodical noted that the ready-made clothing industry's output in 1900 was twenty-two times greater than it was in 1860.[22] The ready-made clothing industry exploded in New York City, where more than $100 million worth of garments were produced in 1900, propelling the United States to become the world leader in ready-made clothing manufacturing. Conversely, the custom dressmaking industry's production decreased from $57 million to $48 million from 1890 to 1900.[23] Women who could afford it could now purchase their entire suite of clothing premade.

American women did not immediately make the change from custom-made to ready-made clothing, however. In a 1927 article titled "Sewing at Home Decreases as 'Ready-Mades' Gain Favor," the *New York Times* cited a study conducted by the US Bureau of Home Economics that found that the sales of dress goods (the various types of fabrics used to make clothing) and women's ready-wear clothing were fairly equal until 1920.[24] For women who were accustomed to clothing themselves within their own homes or within private dressmaking shops, the appeal of ready-made clothing was not enough for them to abandon their traditional, custom-made clothing experience.

Socioeconomic class also played a role in the initial adoption of women's ready-made clothing. Some working-class women continued to make their own clothing because they could not afford ready-made garments.[25] They purchased less expensive fabrics from pushcarts or neighborhood stores and they modeled their style after middle- and upper-class women.[26] Other working-class women purchased cheaper versions of ready-made clothing at lower-end specialty clothing stores, from street vendors, or possibly in a department store "bargain basement."[27] Working-class women also often altered and reworked older clothing through the use of trimmings they purchased from neighborhood peddlers.[28] Thus some women, whether because of tradition, personal preference, or economic reasons, continued to make and alter their own clothing within the private settings of their own homes well into the twentieth century.

Public Place: The Department Store

Clothes shopping became a much more public experience for middle-class women with the rise of the department store. Department store owners and managers, who were major purveyors of ready-made clothing, targeted middle-class women whose leisure time and family income allowed them to freely participate in the growing consumer culture of the late nineteenth century. As middle-class women gained control over the private home environment, they were also called on to shop for and purchase items to furnish their homes and take care of their families.[29] New consumer products, including ready-made clothing, enabled middle-class households to become more reliant on consumption than on production.[30] One contemporary commentator noted that "housekeeping is getting to be ready made, as well as clothing," highlighting the beginnings of an emerging consumption-based middle-class home.[31] Shopping became central to middle-class women's role within the household in the late nineteenth century.[32] As less emphasis was placed on middle-class women's production of household goods (such as clothing) for their families and themselves, they bought into this growing consumer culture and became central figures in its success.

And the rise of the department store facilitated this shift in middle-class American life. Although department stores began to develop in France between the 1840s and 1860s, American department stores didn't truly begin their ascendance until the 1870s and 1880s.[33] As historian William Leach has noted, American department stores were distinctive for the speed and scope of their expansion during this time, as well as their "prolific middle classness."[34] The department store emerged as an essential site where these consumption-focused middle-class women could shop for and purchase their own clothing as well.

Department stores often began as dry goods stores—purveyors of textiles, fabrics, and related items.[35] Women once shopped at dry goods stores such as Strawbridge & Clothier and Marshall Field's for the fabrics they used to sew their own and their families' clothing.[36] When ready-made women's clothing was introduced, dry goods stores appeared as appropriate retailers because of their established association with dress and sewing goods.

Retail executives and store designers soon realized they needed to create a space that offered middle-class women bodily privacy, where they could try on new ready-made clothing within the department store. To transition the clothing experience of middle-class women from the private home or dressmaker's shop to the department store in the 1890s, store executives understood that they would need to attempt to re-create women's traditional clothing experiences within their stores.

Fitting rooms were initially created to offer bodily privacy, while also referencing the private, domestic interiors of the middle-class home in the vast public space of developing department stores. As Susan Porter Benson argues in *Counter Cultures: Saleswomen, Managers, and Customers in American Department Stores, 1890–1940*, the large scale and the wide range of goods (divided into autonomous departments) offered by the department store distinguished this new type of store from the earlier dry goods stores.[37] Although a larger store expanded the range of available goods (including clothing), it could also lead to an overwhelming experience for middle-class female shoppers, who were used to purchasing or making clothing in more intimate and private settings. A comparison of the departments shown on the first floor of Strawbridge & Clothier in 1876 (Figure 2.1) with the departments shown in 1887 (Figure 2.2) exemplifies this point.

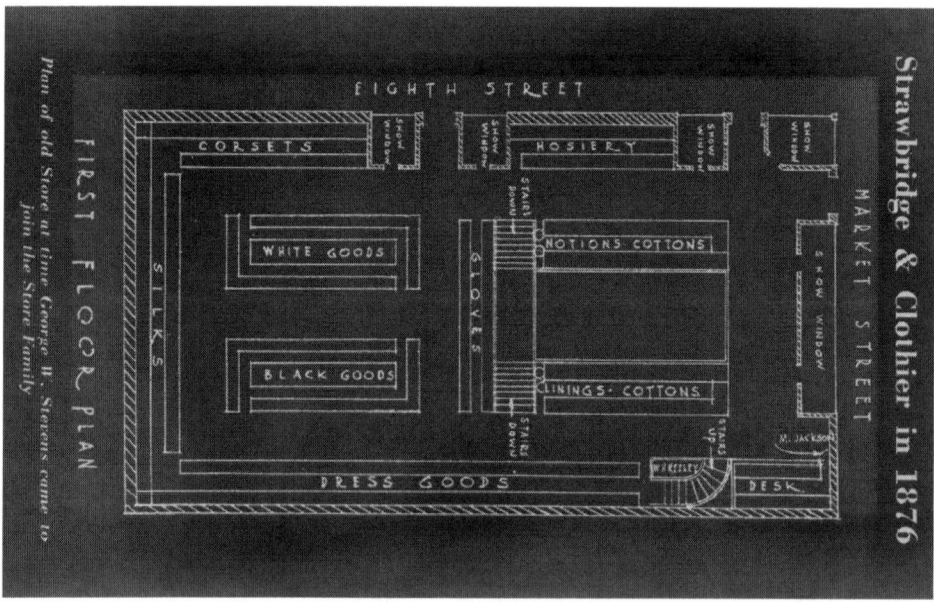

Figure 2.1. "Strawbridge & Clothier in 1876." Strawbridge & Clothier Archive, Accn. 2117, Series V Real Estate Records, Box 33, Manuscripts and Archives, Hagley Museum and Library. Courtesy of Hagley Museum and Library.

Department Store Fitting Rooms   17

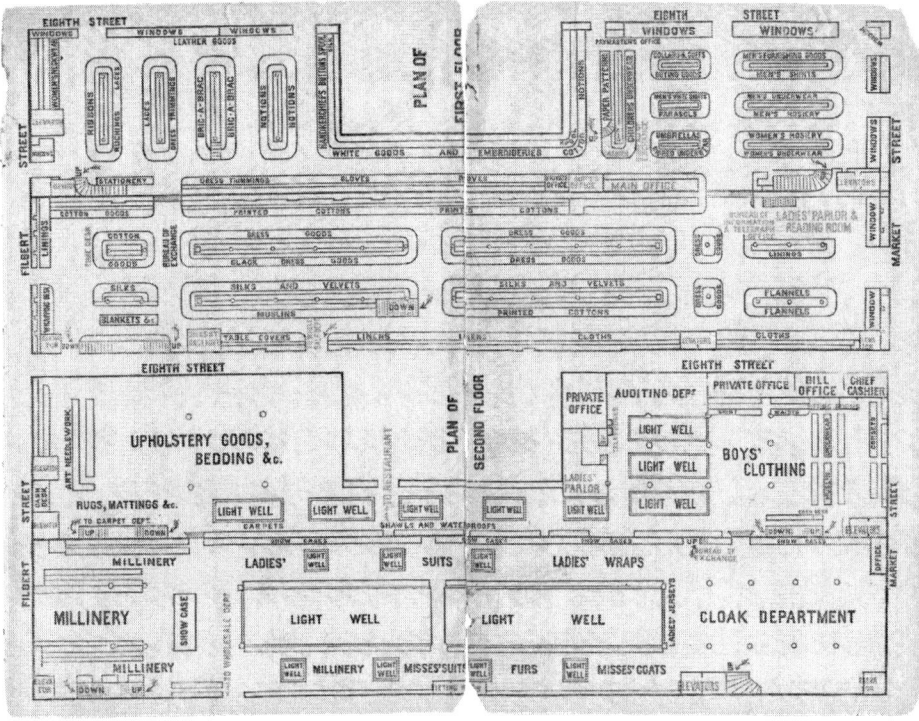

Figure 2.2. "S&C Floorplan of Philadelphia Store," 1887. Strawbridge & Clothier Archive, Accn. 2117, Series V Real Estate Records, Box 33, Manuscripts and Archives, Hagley Museum and Library. Courtesy of Hagley Museum and Library.

In 1876, the first floor consisted of departments for corsets, silks, dress goods, gloves, white and black goods (or white and black dress fabrics), notions (sewing needles, thread, etc.), cottons, linings, and hosiery. By 1887, the store had expanded to include departments devoted to leather goods, women's neckwear (such as collars), ribbons, laces, dress trimmings, bric-a-brac, handkerchiefs, embroideries, paper patterns, umbrellas, ribbed underwear, children's underwear, men's shirts, collars and cuffs, women's and men's underwear and hosiery, blankets, and table covers. While fabrics and materials for making clothing still covered most of the first floor in 1887, ready-made women's coats, suits, and hats had appeared on the second floor. The amount of space on the first and second floors devoted to ready-made goods in 1887 was approximately equal to the floor space devoted to dress goods and other materials for making clothing. This comparison highlights the transition from custom-made to ready-made clothing that occurred during the late nineteenth century. New service spaces such as a wrapping desk, bureau of exchange, bureau of information, and telegraph office also appeared on the first floor of the 1887 store. These spaces offered services that were not associated with the home but that added to the comfort and convenience of department store shopping.[38]

This increase in departments and store offerings was possible only with the growth of the physical space of the store itself. These vast spaces obviously differed greatly from the private and small-scale domestic environments within which women were accustomed to making or buying their clothing. Strawbridge & Clothier, for instance, went through a number of expansions between 1868 and 1928, when an entirely new store was built.[39] By then, Strawbridge & Clothier's main store covered more than twelve acres of floor space.[40] In 1911, Wanamaker's proclaimed that its Philadelphia store was "the largest building in the world devoted to retail merchandizing [sic], occupy[ing] an entire city block ... cover[ing] an area of 250 feet wide, 480 feet long and rising to a height of 247 feet above the sidewalk."[41] In order to construct the Macy's New York store in 1902, thirty-two buildings were torn down to make way for an eventual 23½ acres of floor space.[42] Not only did department stores become larger in scale, they also became more elaborate. Many stores established large central courts or grand staircases that would greet department store customers when they arrived. Smaller goods such as jewelry and other accessories were often placed behind elaborate counters and cabinets where access could be completely controlled by saleswomen. Larger items, like apparel, were often placed on large tables and racks, allowing customers greater access, but always under the supervision of saleswomen.[43] For American female shoppers who used to purchase or make their clothing in more traditional settings, these grand department stores had the potential to overwhelm and intimidate, at least according to department store executives.

Designers and owners sought to create spaces that offered bodily privacy within the large, public department store to mitigate the overpowering effect of these massive spaces. The 1887 floor plan depicting the Philadelphia Strawbridge & Clothier store (see Figure 2.2) demonstrates store owners' quest to re-create the intimate experience associated with earlier clothing experiences. This floor plan, which lacks the measurements or details that a professional floor plan would contain, appears to have been created for customers to familiarize themselves with the store's new layout following the 1887 addition of sixty-five feet of store frontage on Market Street.[44]

Documents such as these floor plans helped customers become acclimated to a new environment. The floor plan was folded down the middle and may have been placed within a periodical of some sort. The title "What We Look Like," printed on the reverse side of the floor plan, communicated an air of friendliness that department store executives wanted to convey (Figure 2.3). Furthermore, the paper used for the cover page was embossed to look like white satin wallpaper, echoing the interiors of shoppers' homes. Floor plans such as this one created a sense of familiarity with the department store while directing customers through the space. The floor plan highlights department store executives' quest to re-create the bodily privacy middle-class women had previously experienced in their homes or at dressmakers' shops.

Gender segregation also became an important way to offer women bodily privacy in the department store. A closer look at the floor plan itself (see Figure 2.2) reveals the bounding and restricting of the women's clothing

Figure 2.3. "S&C Floorplan of Philadelphia Store," 1887 (reverse side). Strawbridge & Clothier Archive, Accn. 2117, Series V Real Estate Records, Box 33, Manuscripts and Archives, Hagley Museum and Library. Courtesy of Hagley Museum and Library.

area of the store. After entering the store from Market Street, the female shopper could turn right and find herself in the "Ladies' Parlor and Reading Room." From here, she could ascend a staircase to the second floor, above all the busy foot traffic of the main floor below, to the "Cloak Department" with a "Ladies Jersey's" section toward the far side. After passing through "Misses' Coats" and "Furs," the female customer arrives at the "Misses' Suits" department. The department contained a set of "Fitting Rooms" tucked away against the far wall of the store. The title "Fitting Room" was highlighted in red lettering, making it stand out against the black lines and text throughout the floor plan. The red lettering likely allowed customers to easily find such service spaces such as elevators and offices, but the text color also drew attention to the placement of the fitting rooms in a secluded, private area of the store.

Creating Privacy in Public: Physical Design

Department store designers and executives recognized that they needed to find a way to provide bodily privacy within the new space of the public department store for women to accept this fundamental shift away from their traditional clothing experience. Store executives and managers sought to create a private, intimate space within this site where female shoppers would feel comfortable trying on new, ready-made clothing. The department store fitting room (or "dressing room") formed the central space to experience this privacy in public.

The need for bodily privacy increased as ready-made clothing rose to dominate the department store's offerings. As ready-made clothing increased in popularity, women needed private spaces to try on these premade garments. Dressing rooms or fitting rooms emerged as sites dedicated to providing privacy within the public space of the department stores. "Fitting rooms, the decorations and furnishings of which were much more ornate than those of miladi's chamber in a royal palace, sprang up" to facilitate, and perhaps influence, the changing needs of female shoppers.[45] Fitting rooms came to be the "usual" provision in the "ready-to-wear department."[46]

The physical space of these new fitting rooms was designed to afford bodily privacy and space to examine the fit of ready-made clothing. Typical fitting rooms were six square feet with a full-length mirror.[47] Some of the more elaborately furnished rooms offered "duplicate mirrors, arranged so that they can be turned at an angle, both perpendicularly and horizontally, thereby enabling the customer to obtain a perfect view of the merchandise she may be trying on."[48] Another store offered dressing rooms "with special lighting fixtures . . . so that the customers can have the same advantage in choosing their goods as they would in the out-of-doors-light."[49]

The Robert Fraser Department Store in Utica, New York, offered an exemplary women's clothing department (Figure 2.4). Women's clothing and shoe departments were isolated on the second floor. The ready-made suit and cloak section was "regarded as one of the show features of the Fraser store" and was "fitted up with exceptional elegance."[50] The "handsomely appointed" fitting rooms were decorated with elaborate woodwork and featured two full-length mirrors positioned at a thirty-five-degree angle, "affording a better view of the garment when being tried on."[51] The fitting rooms were apparently a popular feature with female costumers, as triplicate mirrors attached to the garment cabinets were utilized when the fitting rooms were "overcrowded."[52]

The isolation of the Fraser store fitting rooms highlights one of the most essential ways to offer a body privacy: to completely hide it from view, which would become one of the most important design features of these emerging

Figure 2.4. Section of Garment Department, Robert Fraser, Utica, New York, from "Simple Elegance the Keynote," *Dry Goods Economist* (April 27, 1907): 95. Courtesy of the Library of Congress.

spaces. Women's fitting rooms needed to be placed within the women's clothing department, allowing women trying on clothing to be shielded from random passersby and, more specifically, from men who did not "belong" in the women's clothing section. In another example, the Espenhain Dry Goods Co. Store in Milwaukee screened its women's fitting rooms by placing them behind garment showcases, similar to a proposed floor plan in the *Dry Goods Economist* (Figure 2.5).

Store executives sought to re-create earlier clothing experiences by strictly segregating spaces for men and women, especially the highly private areas of the fitting rooms. Designers placed fitting rooms in discreet locations that were gender exclusive and visually hidden. Women's fitting rooms were typically located within women's clothing departments, often along exterior walls on upper floors. This location enabled the gender segregation of users by placing fitting rooms within gender-restricted areas of the store. Placing the room along an exterior wall also allowed fitting rooms to be located in lower-traffic areas with less visibility.

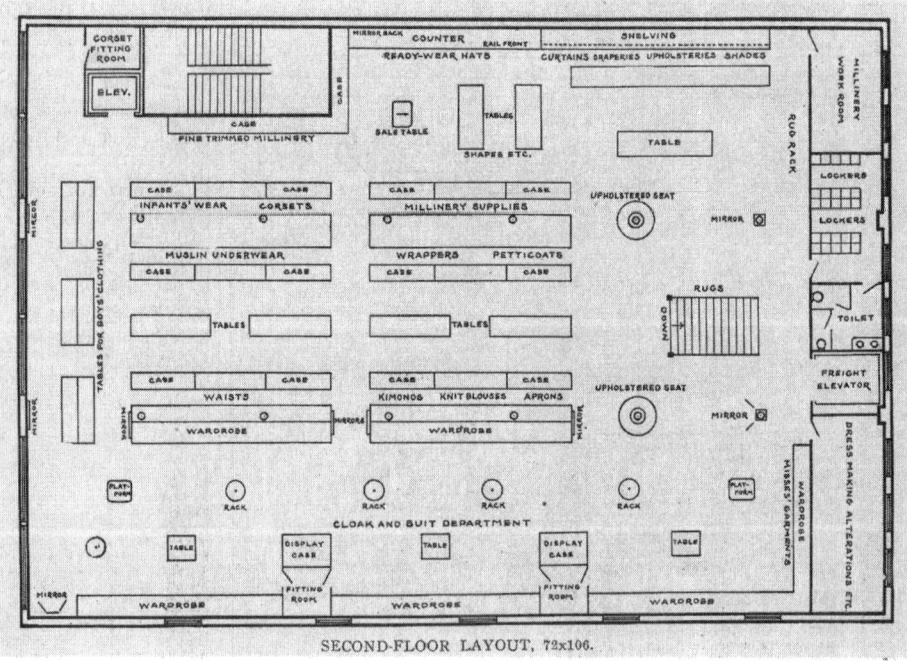

Figure 2.5. "Second-Floor Layout," from "Store Arrangement," *Dry Goods Economist* (November 24, 1906): 59. Courtesy of the Library of Congress.

Indeed, fitting rooms provided an important space for department store owners and executives to create bodily privacy in public. "Women," noted one commentator, "like seclusion in the selection of their wearing apparel."[53] Thus, the placement, design, and furnishings of fitting rooms were given extensive consideration. The advertisers for the Simpson Crawford Company department store extolled the store's fitting rooms in 1902 as "so arranged that they can be shut off from all the others, thus insuring perfect privacy when desired."[54]

In order to further seclude the women's clothing section, most department store floor plans placed women's ready-made clothing departments and fitting rooms on upper floors instead of the first floor, as in the Marshall Field store in Chicago and the William Doerflinger Co. Store in La Crosse, Wisconsin (Figure 2.6).[55]

In these examples, female customers had their own private upper floor. Certainly store executives had practical reasons to move women's clothing off the ground floor. To facilitate foot traffic on the ground floor, one text suggested "to those upper floors go the folk whose purchases necessitate the fitting of something or other to the human frame."[56] The author held up Macy's in New York as a prime example: "On the third [floor] is the women's

Figure 2.6. Women's cloak and suit department in the William Doerflinger Co. Store in La Crosse, Wisconsin, from "New Fixtures the Factor," *Dry Goods Economist* (June 23, 1906): 5. Courtesy of the Library of Congress.

wearing apparel, with special dressing-room facilities for trying on and fitting."[57] Retailers also believed that female shoppers could "more easily be persuaded to ascend a flight of stairs in search of merchandise which they need than men."[58] For their part, men seemed to prefer this gender segregation as well. One store owner contemplated creating two entrances for his store, because the majority of his "men customers [did] not care to go through the ladies departments."[59]

This placement also echoed the private spaces of the late nineteenth-century home, with private bedrooms placed on the upper floors and public spaces, such as parlors, on the first floor. The fitting rooms were also placed within women's clothing departments (usually along a wall or in a corner), instead of in the middle of a floor or in a separate section. The editors of the trade journal *Dry Goods Economist* recommended that the women's ready-made clothing department, with its "skirt racks, mirrors, and fitting-room," be "entirely distinct from the rest of the store."[60] The November 23, 1912, edition of the journal suggested floor plans for the first and second floors of a department store (Figure 2.7).

In an accompanying article, the author called for the "department featuring misses' garments" to be "honored with a separate alcove section [of fitting rooms]" in a portion of the article titled "Arrangement of Fitting Rooms."[61] According to the editors of the *Dry Goods Economist*, women's toilets and restrooms, along with fitting rooms, "naturally belonged in the rear" of the second floor.[62] Another proposed department store layout appeared in a 1905 edition of the journal and suggested that women's fitting rooms could be discreetly covered with clothing wardrobes while still retaining their "convenience" and "abundant lighting."[63] The authors of the floor plans and articles called for clearly delineated gendered spaces.

As department stores began to expand their amenities, store designers and executives continued to segregate space according to gender. Some stores located their women's fitting rooms within the women's clothing department, close to ladies' parlors or lounges (often equipped with toilet facilities), to enhance the female shopper's experience of privacy within the store.[64] According to one department store owner, "no modern store is complete nowadays without a rest and retiring room for women, and we have found it one of the best investments we ever made."[65] The editors of the *Dry Goods Economist* declared that "a cleanly, well-equipped women's toilet is not only a necessity but an excellent investment for any modern store."[66] The placement of the fitting rooms within the shelter of the women's clothing depart-

Department Store Fitting Rooms 25

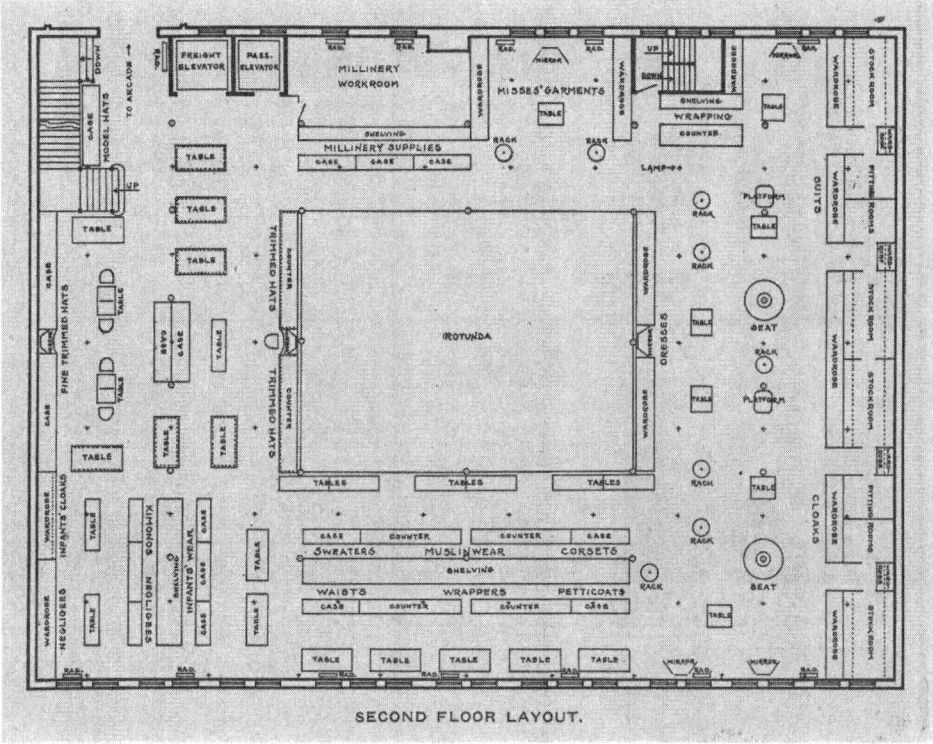

Figure 2.7. "Second Floor Layout," from "Two Floor Layouts," *Dry Goods Economist* 67, no. 3568 (November 23, 1912): 13. Courtesy of the Library of Congress.

ment on the upper floors of the department store created an intimate, private space within the large public department store.

Department store owners were even encouraged to offer different classes of fitting rooms "in order to give . . . more exclusive customers who may be inspecting extra fine costumes the best possible all-round view of the garments."[67] Although most department store customers were middle-class women, these women were, at times, further divided according to economic level within the segregated women's section of the store.

The physical designs of these early fitting rooms can be "read" as evidence of middle-class conceptions of privacy at this time. The designers and creators of these spaces materially manifested their understanding of privacy as fundamentally gender segregated. This is apparent in the labeling of the spaces as belonging to "ladies" and the placement of the rooms in progressively more gendered, secluded, and separated areas of the store. These emerging designs were physically constructed to reflect social understandings of what constituted private space; thus, they were not only physically but also socially constructed.

Creating Privacy in Public: Social Construction

The physical gender separation within the department store reflected middle-class society's definition of bodily privacy. Store managers and owners further defined privacy within their stores by creating a gendered division of spaces. The arrangement of displays often physically separated men and women as they entered the department store. In a series of weekly articles on model department store arrangements, the editors of *Dry Goods Economist* argued that menswear items should ideally be placed near the entrance of the store and in a separate area from women's clothing or accessories.[68] In a proposed floor plan, the journal's editors "endeavored to keep the goods . . . for the two sexes in sections of the store which are entirely separate."[69] And, in 1905, the journal's editors counseled a department store owner to place "men's furnishings just inside the entrance . . . where they can be reached without the necessity of passing through the departments carrying women's goods exclusively."[70] In fact, the editors of the *Dry Goods Economist* commended one retailer for placing menswear items near the grocery section of the store, so "the men will not be embarrassed by having to pass through the women's departments in order to reach any goods they may be seeking."[71] Alternatively, boys' clothing could be located near the men's department and "placed where it can be examined by the women without need of their passing the men's department," implying that mothers, not fathers, were responsible for acquiring clothing for their sons.[72] Store executives even contemplated segregating the shoe department by gender through the use of a display case, thus offering "the necessary seclusion to the women's end."[73]

This gender separation suggests that department store executives (who were likely middle- to upper-class men) sought to re-create the female relationships and private spaces traditionally associated with women's clothing within the department store (Figure 2.8). In the Strawbridge & Clothier store floor plan from 1887 (see Figure 2.2), a "Ladies' Parlor and Reading Room" is located near the dress goods area. This placement allowed women to move within adjacent gendered spaces without having to pass through any areas where men might also be shopping. Editors of the *Dry Goods Economist* hoped that store owners and managers would recognize the value of designing their stores so that customers would not need to pass "through depart-

Figure 2.8. "Suit Section: Store of L. S. Ayers & Co., Indianapolis," from "Cloaks and Suits," *Dry Goods Economist* (February 9, 1907): 55. Courtesy of the Library of Congress.

ments devoted to the sale of merchandise which is almost exclusively sold to the opposite sex." As one author noted, "this feature in the layout [of the store] will contribute quite materially to a larger business."[74]

This social construction of bodily privacy is reflected in the physical arrangement of these early department stores. The basement plan from Wanamaker's 1887 Philadelphia store directory shows a "Ladies' Waiting Room" separated by a wall from the "Gentlemen's Waiting Room" (Figure 2.9). These spaces were apparently provided for men and women to wait for each other after they had finished shopping in their separate sections of the store.[75] Also, the placement of the waiting rooms near the toy and musical instrument departments allowed men and women access to their respective waiting rooms without passing through spaces circumscribed to a different gender. In the *Dry Goods Economist*'s suggested floor plan in Figure 2.7, the entire second floor is devoted to women's clothing. In 1878, the Stern Brothers' New York dry goods store advertised its move to a larger building in *The Independent*, making sure that prospective customers were aware that the store's second floor "contains a class of goods very interesting to the ladies—namely ladies costumes, cloaks, wraps, and shawls, furs," as well as "ladies' reception and fitting rooms."[76] One department store owner was cautioned against building a fountain on the second floor of his store because "women customers would prefer the convenience and quiet of a restroom, to the more conspicuous location near the fountain."[77]

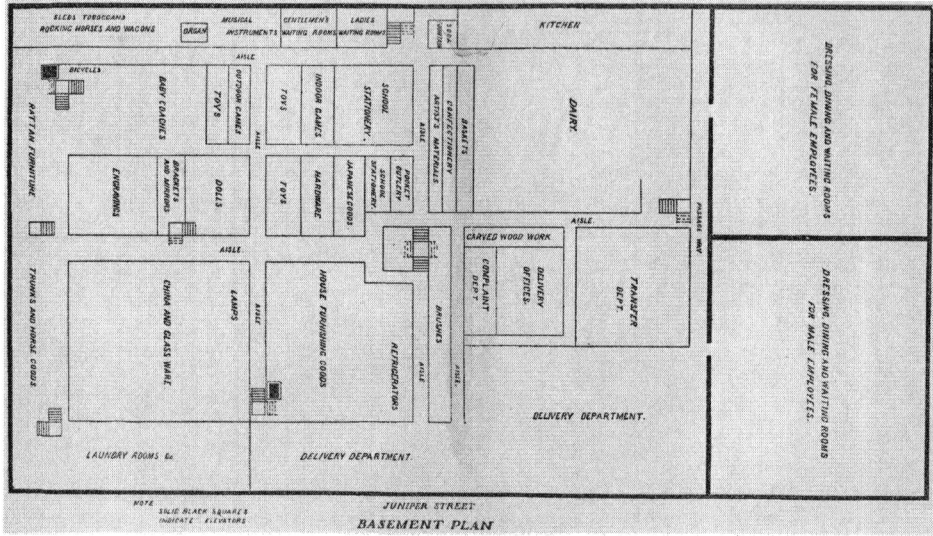

Figure 2.9. "Basement Plan," from *The Wanamaker Store Directory*, 1887. Courtesy of Hagley Museum and Library.

But by placing these spaces on an upper floor, women could also browse, try on, and purchase clothing within a segregated, private space that had been secured from possible male intrusion by dividing these spaces along gender lines. One store placed a "layette room" on the third floor so that "prospective mothers can shop in seclusion."[78] The implication here is that the pregnant female body required seclusion and increased privacy within the store. This layette room was situated near "a children's barber shop, beauty parlors, hair dressing room, and a rest room . . . [and] an alteration room for all ready-to-wear, as well as the needed fitting rooms."[79]

It appears that men and women heeded this gender separation when they entered the department store. One Strawbridge & Clothier employee recounted a scene that she "frequently" saw in the store's waiting room. A man "stamped up and down, furiously chewed his moustache, . . . and every few minutes consulted his watch," as he waited for his wife. She later appeared "hurried and worried" at the prospect of having made her husband wait. Her excuse? "'Well, the dressmaker—.'"[80] Men and women, even if they were married, did not appear to accompany each other into gender-segregated areas of the department store. These waiting rooms were commonly placed in gender-neutral locations so that men and women could enter them from areas not separated by gender (although women may have been granted access to men's clothing departments if they were shopping for their husbands or relatives). Patrons appear to have respected the public privacy created by the department store designers, owners, and managers.

In addition to creating private spaces within the public department store, managers and owners sought to create a welcoming environment in which women would be comfortable with performing the private, intimate activity of clothing themselves. The editors of the *Dry Goods Economist* advocated dividing women's ready-made clothing departments according to size and quality, allowing for "a certain amount of privacy [for] purchasers ... [as] there are occasions when this opportunity will be appreciated."[81] According to the editors, "a woman who has about decided upon purchasing a low-priced garment will not be upset in her decision by seeing a higher-priced garment being shown to a more wealthy customer in an adjoining alcove."[82] Working-class women were often directed toward less expensive, less elaborately decorated areas of the store.[83] In Wanamaker's advertisements from the late 1890s, store executives emphasized "comfortable" and "cozy" fitting rooms that were "conveniently located."[84] For the opening of a new store, H. O'Neill & Company advertised "more commodious quarters, with their elegant surroundings and fine large fitting rooms, you will find it a pleasure to consider your Fall selections."[85] Advertisers attempted to coax women out of the private space of the home by reassuring female customers that they would be comfortable in the new space of the department store. As the H. O'Neill & Company advertisement continued, the new store boasted "broad aisles, enlarged and conveniently arranged departments ... to make shopping today quick, methodical, comfortable and pleasant."[86] This evidence suggests that women needed to be persuaded to move their clothing experiences from the privacy of their home or their personal dressmaker to the public space of the store.

Male customers were also offered spaces to change their clothes, but these rooms were often referred to as "try-on rooms" (Figure 2.10).[87] As this title indicates, male customers were expected to simply try on ready-made clothing to decide whether or not to make a purchase. Rooms where female customers tried on ready-made clothing were often referred to as "fitting rooms," suggesting that women still needed assistance from saleswomen to find the correct fit. The title "fitting room" also linked these new spaces of public privacy with earlier fitting rooms located in private dressmaking shops.

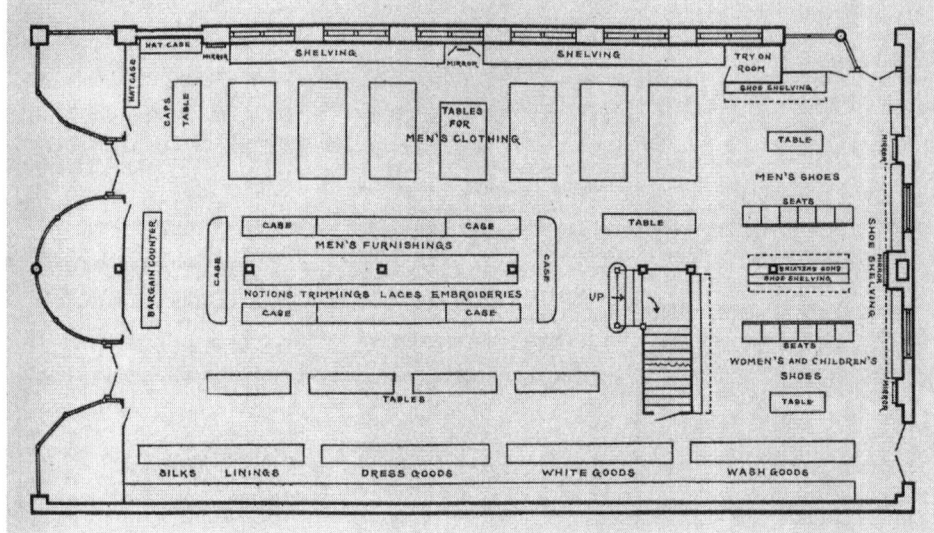

Figure 2.10. From "Store Arrangement," *Dry Goods Economist* (July 15, 1905): 91. Courtesy of the Library of Congress.

In linking the social construction and the physical design of early fitting rooms, we can learn why these sites took the form they did. Store managers, designers, and executives created private spaces in public department stores by adhering to their social understanding of privacy. Accordingly, undressed bodies needed to be hidden from public view. And, most important, male and female bodies needed to be physically and visually separated.

Creating Privacy in Public: The Human Element

Department store executives and designers went to great lengths to create physically private spaces by offering fitting rooms in secluded, gender-segregated areas of the store. They also attempted to create domestic connections between the earlier clothing setting through the layout of the store itself and by encouraging close relationships between saleswomen and female customers. However, it was the saleswomen who most reflected the traditional gender segregation associated with earlier clothing experiences. Department store saleswomen were an integral part of the experience of these rooms, strengthening their gendered homogeneity. These saleswomen proved to be an essential component of defining specific store spaces, especially dressing rooms, as private, allowing female customers bodily privacy while dressing and undressing.

Department store executives quickly noted the importance of the customer–sales staff relationship. Stores such as Marshall Field first hired female employees, as opposed to salesmen, to work in women's ready-made clothing departments.[88] A 1913 ad for a showcase company depicted a typical interaction between a customer and saleswoman in the female clothing section of a department store (Figure 2.11). In the photograph, a saleswoman shows a ready-made dress to a customer. If she liked what she saw, the customer would possibly try on the garment in one of the store's fitting rooms with the assistance of the saleswoman before finally purchasing the dress. Alterations were available if the standard sizing of ready-made clothing did not fit a customer correctly.[89] Saleswomen personally ushered female customers through the entire process of clothes shopping. This personal interaction was essential for defining sites of privacy in the department store.

Through their employee periodical, *Store Chat,* Strawbridge & Clothier executives and managers communicated the importance of this relationship directly to their employees. *Store Chat* noted that although "the owners of the business . . . seldom come into contact with the public, the salespeople and a few groups of others are the connecting link, the personal representatives of the owners, the hosts and hostesses of the public."[90] The article declared that

Figure 2.11. Grand Rapids Show Case Company, advertisement from *Dry Goods Economist* 67, no. 3581 (February 22, 1913): 93. Courtesy of the Library of Congress.

"upon [the salespeople] depends the success or failure of the business."[91] Department store managers and executives attempted to influence relations between salespeople and customers through such articles in employee periodicals. Saleswomen were vital to the transition from women's earlier, private, domestic clothing experiences to the more public department store environment.

For customers to "buy into" the privacy that department store executives tried to create, salespeople had to believe in this intimate relationship as well. Indeed, a relationship was founded on the shared gender of the customer and clerk. To that end, Strawbridge & Clothier managers employed the pages of *Store Chat* to market this relationship to their employees. Authors in the periodical referred to salespeople as part of the "Store Family."[92] Strawbridge & Clothier managers called the store "the House," and all customers were "invited guest[s] of the store."[93] If department store executives wanted female customers to truly feel as though they were entering an intimate, comfortable environment, the salespeople would need to act accordingly. Saleswomen, especially, would need to function as surrogate family members or dressmakers for women used to more traditional clothing experiences.

Saleswomen were featured prominently in these publications. The attributes of the ideal saleswoman included "perseverance, earnestness, reliability, sincerity, optimism, naturalness, ability, loyalty, initiative, tidiness, and yearning."[94] The skilled saleswoman also needed a "full knowledge of her work and the quality of goods which she readily and gladly imparts to her customer."[95] One member of the "Store Family" reported on how she succeeded as a saleswoman. She made "every customer feel that [she was] personally interested in them, always greeting them with a smile."[96] The image of the ideal saleswoman emphasized her role in making the customer comfortable and forming a relationship with the customer. One department store even placed the saleswomen's locker room and dressing room on the store's second floor, not far from the customers' fitting rooms, thus creating a gender-segregated floor where customers and saleswomen alike were offered private spaces to change their clothing.[97] By encouraging saleswomen to create a familiarity with their female customers, department store executives attempted to replicate the relationship women traditionally had with their personal dressmakers or family members who had formerly outfitted them (Figure 2.12).

Figure 2.12. "You Can Fit Good-Looking Women with Good-Looking Clothes," from "The Woman's Invasion," *Everybody's Magazine* 20, no. 1 (January 1909): 76. Courtesy of Hathi Trust Digital Library.

But store managers also stressed that this familiarity should not come at the expense of professionalism. Even though customers and saleswomen shared their gender, they were also members of differing classes. One text on store management relayed an anecdote about a struggling store where "customers have come away, vowing that they would never go there again, and their reason when finally discovered was that so many saleswomen on every side were constantly 'fixing' their hair."[98] Because of this lack of professionalism and decorum, one male customer "said he felt as if he ought to retire from the room, as it was evidently a ladies' dressing-room."[99]

The relationship between saleswomen and customers was also based on saleswomen's expertise and knowledge of the female bodies, affording saleswomen another reason to be allowed entry into these newly constructed dressing rooms. The managers of Strawbridge & Clothier, as well as other retailers, stressed the importance of saleswomen's knowledge and expertise in gaining the trust of female shoppers. As one author stated, "it is in the Fitting Room where the art of salesmanship is more fully demonstrated to the ultimate satisfaction of the customer."[100] Saleswomen should be able to "tell when a prospective customer approaches in the Gown and Suit Department just what style and color will be most becoming to her."[101] Strawbridge & Clothier executives wanted their saleswomen to assist female clothes shoppers who "may not have a good eye for color effects, sustainability of materials and styles."[102] Indeed, working-class saleswomen were allowed entry into department store dressing rooms because of their knowledge and understanding of their middle-class customers' needs. It was in this personal relationship between the saleswoman and her customer that the department store's quest to create privacy truly came to fruition. Saleswomen created the vital link between the layout and design of the department store and the store's marketing and advertising campaigns. Thus, privacy within developing department stores was defined most essentially by spatial and social gender segregation.

While the spatial and social segregation created in dressing rooms allowed for bodily privacy, they also unintentionally offered sites for possible transgressive behavior. The privacy of the department store fitting room enabled some saleswomen to defy the lofty goals of the department store managers and executives. In an article entitled "What's to Be Done with the Girl Who Has the Manner but Can't Seem to Sell Goods?," one department store manager bemoaned that one of his saleswomen was a "failure" when it came to assisting customers who were trying on clothing. Out of sight of the floor manager or her supervisor, "she subconsciously felt that the charm of the luxuriously mirrored private dressing room . . . would swing the sale" and "made no effort."[103]

In another anecdote from a contemporary periodical, a department store saleswoman accused a coworker of "stealing the company's time" by lingering in the dressing room and hiding behind dresses in order to avoid her work.[104] While fitting rooms offered customers the necessary privacy to change their clothing in public, these rooms also afforded saleswomen the opportunity to engage in behaviors not sanctioned by department store executives and managers. Editors at the *Dry Goods Economist* also cautioned store owners and managers against offering saleswomen their own connecting toilet and dressing rooms, because "when such rooms adjoin it is usually found that the help are more apt to congregate and loaf in the dressing room."[105]

It was clear that the privacy afforded in the dressing room was essential not only to women's changing of clothing but also to the selling of those clothes. Here, working-class saleswomen and middle-class clients could discuss the merits of specific garments in a visually protected site, far from possible (male) intrusions.

~

Department store dressing rooms were one of the earliest private spaces created in a public place, offering us the opportunity to explore how such sites originated. To understand the socially contested nature of privacy, it is necessary to first understand the physical and social construction of these spaces. Here, the contestation over the meaning of privacy became visible as it entered the public sphere of the developing department store. Department store designers and executives needed to convince their customers (largely middle-class women) that the private act of dressing and undressing their bodies could be performed in a new public place.

As the private space of the home and dressmaker's shop gave way to the very public, much larger department store at the turn of the twentieth century, department store managers and executives sought to create a private space to facilitate this shift for their customers. By creating privacy in spaces such as the department store fitting room, female customers were ushered into a new clothing experience defined by mass-produced, ready-made clothing. Saleswomen stepped in as a substitute for the familiar dressmakers or family members formerly charged with creating women's clothing. Department stores' ultimate success in creating this public privacy is evidenced by their continued growth and their eventual domination of the sale of women's ready-made clothing. Although some American women still make their clothing to this day, many more continue to try on mass-produced clothing within the private space of the department store fitting room.

In the next chapter, we will move from the department store fitting room to our next spatial case study: the public bath. Here, the intended users were mostly working-class, and often immigrants, in contrast to the middle-class women department stores catered to. Just as fitting rooms were designed around the private act of dressing and undressing, public baths were created to enable the private act of bathing to take place in a public place.

CHAPTER THREE

Public Baths
Cleansing the "Classed" Body

For the working-class patrons of a newly created public library in turn-of-the-century Calumet, Michigan, education and enlightenment did not end when they closed their books or newspapers. The mining company executives who paid for the library had included a public bath in the basement of the same building. Here, patrons could improve their bodies as well as their minds. In a newspaper article entitled "A Boon to the Community: The Big Corporations Are Certainly Not All Soulless," a contemporary social commentator noted that the new library and bath were open to all, including "the laborer and his family, who, as long as they behave themselves, will be just as welcome within its walls as the biggest 'boss' in the community." The author then stated that because "cleanliness is next to godliness, it is hoped that those who have not accommodation for bathing at home will avail themselves of these baths for themselves and [their] children." The author also made sure to note that men and women, would, of course, have separate facilities.[1]

The Calumet bath offers an example of a typical public bath from this time. Upon entry, users were immediately ushered down separate staircases according to gender and age. After walking through a group washroom, men had the option of taking a bath or a shower in individual stalls. Women and "children" entered a separate washroom and walked past a room of water closets on the way to individual bath stalls. Stall doors shielded users on both sides of the public bath.

At the turn of the twentieth century, middle-class social reformers, municipal officials, industrial leaders, doctors, and sanitary engineers, concerned with the physical and "moral" cleanliness of the working class, sought to provide bathing facilities to the working class through the creation of public baths. While middle- and upper-class Americans increasingly had access to private bathing facilities within their homes during this time, members of the working class, who were more likely to rent their homes, acquired domestic indoor-bathing facilities and fixtures at a much slower pace.[2] Middle-class reformers sought to improve the rudimentary home bathing techniques of the working class by creating public bathing facilities outside working-class homes where patrons' bathing experiences could be supervised and regulated. These social reformers took up the cause of the public bath movement.[3]

By analyzing the public bath as our next spatial case study, we can see how middle-class designers were able to embed their understandings and expectations of privacy into private spaces in public places designed primarily for working-class, often immigrant users. Unlike the dressing room, which was designed by middle-class designers for middle-class citizens, those who used public baths did not fall into the same class and immigration category as those who designed public baths. Therefore, the public bath provides an opportunity to see how middle-class designers attempted to impose their understanding of privacy on others with less societal power.

This power imbalance is also manifested in the enforcement of middle-class privacy through the surveillance of working-class bodies. Public bath patrons were often subjected to physical inspections, were timed during baths or showers, and were rarely alone while they washed. While middle- and upper-class homes allowed users to bathe completely individually in their newly established bathrooms, public baths were by definition more communal and far less exclusive.

Bathing experiences for middle- and working-class Americans were fairly similar until the late nineteenth century. As members of the middle class were able to acquire indoor, domestic "bathrooms," their understandings of privacy began to shift.

Middle-class social reformers began to advance a public bath movement at approximately the same time. This Progressive-era initiative made it possible for the middle class to directly influence the working class's experience of privacy by designing and creating public baths. Middle-class reformers overtly stated that their goal was to "improve" the hygiene habits of the working class, but the public bath movement also resulted in the simultaneous imposition of a middle-class definition of privacy with respect to the act of bathing. At the same time, middle-class reformers attempted to surveil and control the working-class bathing experience through the space of the public bath. We can begin to understand this shift in the experience of bathing and middle-class understandings of privacy by examining the physical spaces of the public baths. Although these sites have been examined before in relation to the larger public health movement of the time, public baths can also be analyzed as a materialization of shifting privacy norms in the late nineteenth and early twentieth century.

Traditional Bathing Techniques

Most Americans in the eighteenth and nineteenth centuries shared similar experiences of bodily privacy while cleansing their bodies. Through much of the nineteenth century, Americans (including members of various socioeconomic classes) bathed their bodies at home in a movable tub, without running water. Private bathhouses began to appear later, but these were restricted to those who could pay for these exclusive baths. As immigration to the United States increased during the nineteenth century, immigrant groups often brought their traditional bathing rituals with them. As industrial sites developed, employers began to offer their workers (usually men) spaces to wash and bathe after work. These domestic, private, and industrial sites demonstrate how bathing experiences and bathing spaces began to transform toward the end of the nineteenth century.

Traditional Home Bathing

In the eighteenth and nineteenth centuries, many Americans shared a common bathing experience that crossed class lines. Women were usually charged with the task of heating water at a hearth or on a stovetop and filling movable washbasins for household baths.[4] Dean Cole, who grew up in Painesdale, Michigan, during the 1920s, recalled that his mother had a large galvanized tub that she would place in the parlor and fill with water heated on the kitchen stove. Considering the difficulty of this undertaking, bathing for most families usually took place only once a week, and the bath water was often recycled for use by several family members.[5] As Bruce Norden, who grew up in Calumet, Michigan, during the 1910s and 1920s recalled, "once a week, you'd take your bath.... You'd put that big washtub out there ... [and] the oldest [child] would get in the bathtub first. Then it's your turn next."[6] For many nineteenth- and early twentieth-century Americans, their bathing options were "a dish-pan, wash-tub, or the kitchen sink," if they bathed at all.[7]

While these earlier bathing experiences took place within the home, bathing was only partly exclusionary, limiting the experience of bodily privacy.

Bathing took place in common rooms intended for other purposes, such as kitchens or parlors. These rooms were located in the home and, at most, nonfamily members could be excluded. For members of the working class, there may have been even less exclusivity in these spaces if the household took in boarders. Even if families could exclude nonfamily members, intergender and intergenerational bathers likely used the same common space. This method of bathing in a shared, movable tub in a common space began to diverge with a developing, middle-class definition of privacy based on physical and social exclusion.

Ethnically Diverse Bathing Traditions

Variations in these traditional home bathing experiences often appeared along ethnic lines. Immigration to the United States expanded during the late nineteenth and early twentieth centuries, and different ethnic groups carried their bathing traditions with them. These techniques often diverged from the standard movable-basin bathing experience. Some immigrants even created entirely distinct bathing spaces that reflected differing social norms surrounding the process of cleansing the body.

For example, the population of the community surrounding Painesdale, like many industrial communities at this time, was ethnically diverse. Finnish, Cornish, French-Canadian, Irish, Norwegian, Swedish, Croatian, Italian, Hungarian, and Slovenian immigrants had descended on the area to work in the local copper mines.[8] Finnish immigrants were the largest ethnic group in the county in 1910, making up 13 percent of the population. Finns brought with them bathing practices that centered on their traditional bathing space, the sauna.[9] Many Finnish homes in the area boasted traditional Finnish saunas, consisting of a wood-paneled room with a wood-fueled stove covered with rocks and a water source so that water could be thrown on the rocks to produce a steam bath.[10] For Finnish immigrants and their families, a weekly or biweekly sauna constituted their traditional bathing routine.[11]

Consider a typical experience of this bathing tradition as seen through the eyes of a second-generation immigrant. Elnore Saaranen was the daughter of two Finnish immigrants who built a family sauna in their backyard in Painesdale in the 1920s. She recalled using the sauna once a week in the winter and twice a week in the summer. Other families opened up their saunas to the public for a small fee. "They would warm it up [for patrons] the day before, and there was a men's side and a women's side to the dressing area," Elnore recalled. According to Elnore, "men and women went at different times, but families would go together." Elnore remembered going into her family's sauna with her mother and her female friends when she was "a little tot" and having to wash the women's backs. While community saunas often attracted other Finnish immigrants, Elnore noted that several Italian families living in her neighborhood also enjoyed them. Unlike more modern saunas, there was no shower attached to these saunas, so the steam was their only method of bathing.[12] Traditionally, sauna bathers used small bundles of birch sticks to cleanse their skin, but soap and water were also used.[13] By the early twentieth century, Finnish-American saunas appear to have been gender segregated, as in the case of Elnore's family. But in the late nineteenth and early twentieth centuries, many rural communities in Finland during this time offered communal, joint saunas for unrelated men and women. Although this practice diminished during the course of the twentieth century, many Finnish families continued to sauna together across gender lines.[14] The Finnish sauna tradition seems to have been assimilated to American life by the 1910s or 1920s, as these saunas were commonly gender segregated and continue to be to this day.

Private Bathhouses

Bathhouses predate public baths as early examples of spaces to bathe outside of the home. Bathing in a bathhouse was more public and more communal, as unrelated adults used these spaces together. These sites have an extensive history dating back to the Roman era. Bathhouses did begin to appear in urban areas of the United States by the nineteenth century, but these were considered "private" bathhouses because customers had to pay to use them. Here we can see that the exclusive use of these spaces relied on socioeconomic status. The privacy afforded patrons of these public spaces depended on users' ability to pay for their bath. The admission or membership charges excluded anyone outside of the upper or middle class from entering these sites. Private bathhouses were also unique in their lavish interiors and the luxurious services offered there.

The Fleischman Baths, for example, were located in the Bryant Park building in New York at the turn of the twentieth century and offered customers a luxurious (and exclusive) bathing experience. For $1.50, patrons could enjoy a variety of baths, including Turkish, electric light, douche, Russian, and plunge baths (Figure 3.1).[15] Patrons were also offered massages, manicures, pedicures, and shampoo service from bathhouse attendants in clean white leotards, as depicted in Figure 3.1. Although initially the baths seem to have

Figure 3.1. "Russian Bath," from *The Fleischman Baths* (New York: Joseph Fleischman, 1908). Courtesy of the New-York Historical Society.

been restricted to men, a later insert in the bath's brochure identified days and times when the bath would be open exclusively for women. But for most working-class men and women, such amenities were far beyond their reach. Although this bathing experience took place outside the private home, upper-class bathhouse patrons could self-select their bathing companions by paying to exclude people from other socioeconomic classes. These private bathhouses were gender segregated, excluding men or women when the other group was present.

Industrial Bathing

Bathing experiences for the working class also changed with the dawn of industrialization. During the Industrial Revolution, there was an overall growth in the population of factory workers in the United States. Owners of some factories and industrial workplaces began to offer baths or change houses (also known as dry houses) for employees. According to one industrial journalist at the time, "in many up-to-date factories shower-baths and lockers are provided for men on the theory that . . . workmen are human and the better-dressed and cleaner an employee is, the greater asset he is to the business."[16] As Elnore Saaranen and Dean and Walter Cole (also children of immigrant copper miners) recalled, their fathers bathed before returning home from work in the local copper mine in a dry house provided by the company. "My dad always came home clean," remembered Walter Cole.[17]

Industrial bathing facilities did not explicitly segregate by gender like earlier private bathhouses and later public bath facilities, because most industrial workers were male. It is important to note, however, that managerial staff often bathed separately from the workers, as evidenced in the change house at the Baltic Mine (Figure 3.2). These sites were implicitly male-only, and laborers were excluded from using facilities reserved for managers.

Workers at the Baltic Mine could utilize tub baths, which afforded some privacy with dividing walls and a door. Individual shower stalls were also available. Other men might have settled for a quick wash-up at a communal washing trough. The Baltic Mine change house, like many others, was equipped with lockers for workers to store a change of clothes and other items. Industrial bathing facilities enabled the workforce to wash at work before returning home. Mining companies and other industrial owners could avoid building bathrooms in individual working-class homes by providing bathing facilities in the workplace.[18]

In addition to offering working-class bathers new spaces dedicated to bathing and cleansing one's body, early change houses also introduced workers to the experience of bathing under surveillance. Attendants or "watchmen" were "kept on duty all the time."[19] The placement of a watchman in these spaces implies that company executives wanted to prevent theft or other transgressions. This surveillance limited the experience of privacy for factory workers bathing away from home. And it marks an essential distinction between middle- and working-class experiences of bathing during this time. Change houses allowed for increased gender and class exclusion, but middle-class managers and executives felt the need to closely monitor and regulate these new spaces. As we will see, these spaces served as important precursors to later public baths.

Bathing at Home: Dedicated "Bath" Rooms

As mentioned earlier, prior to the mid-nineteenth century, many Americans shared a similar bathing routine: a movable-basin bath or a sponge bath in a common space (such as a kitchen or parlor) within the home.[20] The middle-class bathing experience began to change at the end of the nineteenth century as distinct home "bathrooms" became available to those who could afford

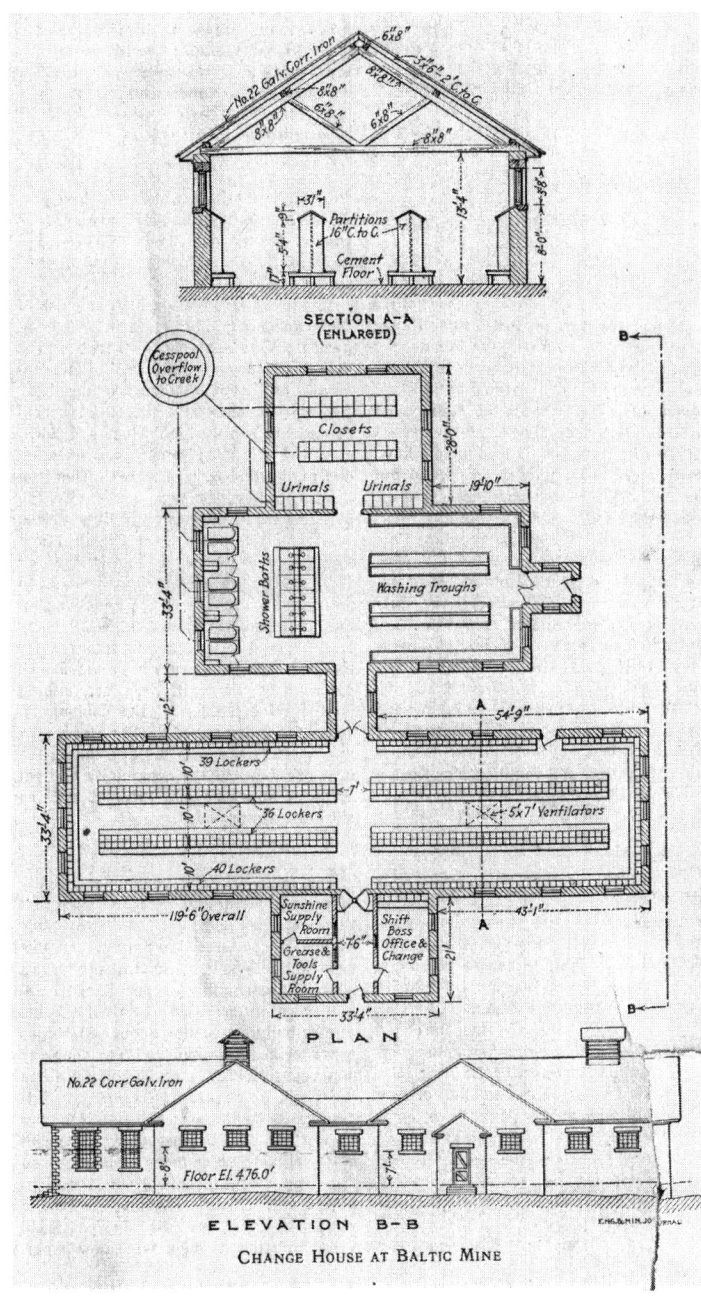

Figure 3.2. "Change House at Baltic Mine," from "Labor Conditions at Copper Range," *Engineering and Mining Journal* 94, no. 26 (December 28, 1912): 1230. Courtesy of the Michigan Technological University Library.

them. Improvements in plumbing technology, changes in cultural understandings of health and hygiene, and a shift in the social value of cleanliness combined to give daily bathing a new importance in the late nineteenth century. Advances in plumbing technology allowed municipal water systems to expand to meet the needs of the growing, urbanizing, and industrializing American population.[21] Upper- and middle-class Americans had the means to build new houses or remodel existing ones to connect to these developing water systems. The middle-class American home came to include dedicated bathrooms, as built-in bathtubs, sinks, and toilets replaced movable tubs and outdoor privies.[22] Members of the middle and upper classes utilized these changes to craft a new space and process for cleansing their bodies. Figure 3.3, entitled "Everything Right in a Bathroom," glorifies the three-piece private bathroom that was becoming standard in middle-class homes. The image features shiny, white, clean surfaces in a light and airy bathroom. Published in *Community Hygiene* in 1916, this bathroom exemplifies the ideal sanitary, hygienic, and private middle-class bathing experience at that time.

Members of the working class took much longer to acquire dedicated three-piece bathrooms in their homes. Indoor plumbing and plumbing fixtures appeared much more slowly in working-class housing, and traditional bathing experiences in movable tubs persisted even as middle-class bathing options were expanding.[23] Cost and lack of space meant that working-class homes often acquired toilets and fixed sinks and baths in a piecemeal fashion. Sinks, toilets, and baths were often added at different times and in spaces other than dedicated bathrooms.[24] For instance, in houses built by mining companies in Painesdale and the surrounding communities, single toilets were initially retrofitted into basements instead of having a dedicated bathroom.[25] In 1897, New York's Committee on Public Baths and Public Comfort Stations reported that at least 90 percent of the houses and tenements in Baltimore, Chicago, New York, and Philadelphia did not have dedicated private bathrooms.[26]

Middle-class Americans developed different expectations of bodily privacy while cleansing their bodies in their own home bathrooms. Users could be completely alone within their own home while bathing their body in total isolation from others. These spaces offered the most exclusive experience of privacy possible; social segregation could be taken to the extreme because these bathrooms were designed for only one user at a time. Through the creation of private bathroom spaces within their own homes, members of the middle class were also able to redefine the private activity of bathing

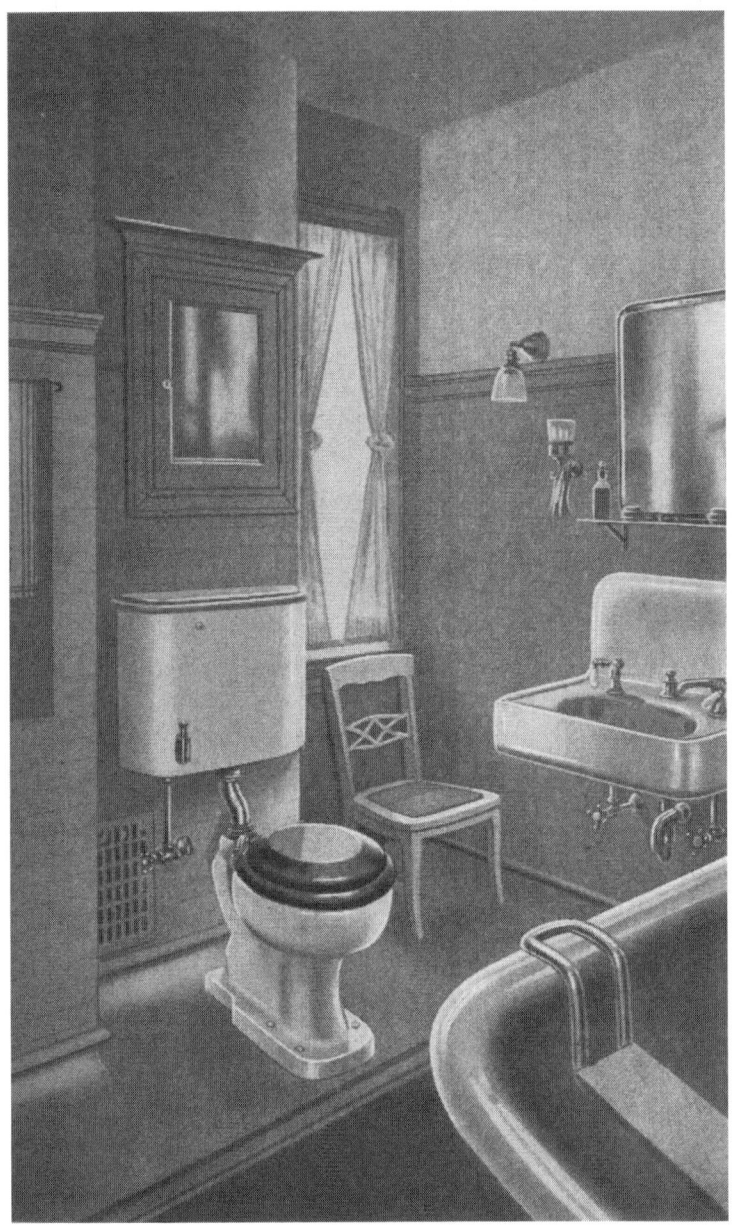

Figure 3.3. "Everything Right in a Bathroom," in Woods Hutchinson, *Community Hygiene* (New York: Houghton Mifflin, 1916), 59. Courtesy of Hathi Trust Digital Library.

one's body. "Proper" bathing came to be defined as washing one's body daily with soap and water. This redefinition of privacy and the private act of bathing allowed middle-class Americans to solidify their social status as distinct from those without dedicated, private bathrooms.

Middle-class reformers with access to dedicated bathrooms began to consider bathing in a movable basin temporarily placed in a common area as problematic. This traditional bathing method no longer aligned with middle-class expectations of proper, private bathing. There was certainly a lack of exclusion, considering there was no single, discrete room dedicated to bathing. This led to potential intergenerational and intergender encounters within family units during bath times. In addition, recycling water from one family member to the next was not considered hygienic to middle-class reformers residing in homes with running water and a dedicated bathroom.

Members of the upper and middle classes used their access to new, exclusive bathrooms to conflate bathing and hygiene with class status.[27] Despite being gender segregated, the Finnish immigrant sauna and other ethnic bathing techniques were not in line with the new middle-class experience of cleansing one's body in a dedicated bathroom. Contemporary reformers concluded that a sweat bath would simply not do. A soap-and-water bath or shower was the only acceptable means of cleansing one's body, according to social commentators. By keeping their bodies clean with daily baths and showers with running water, middle-class Americans demonstrated their respectability and decency.[28] Their ability to exclude all others from this process established a newfound experience of privacy while bathing. Since working-class Americans did not have the same access to private bathing facilities, members of the middle class were able to distinguish themselves as socially, morally, and hygienically superior to the working class.[29]

Imposing Hygiene: The Public Bath Movement

Middle-class social activists developed a "public bath movement" during the turn of the twentieth century to impose their new expectations regarding bathing and privacy onto the working class. The history of this movement is essential to understanding the impetus for the emerging space of the public bath at this time. City officials, journalists, and public health proponents engaged in a lively discourse regarding the creation and implementation of public baths, leaving a trail of documentary evidence. But this evidence offers only part of the story. By interrogating the physical evidence of these spaces, we can see that the middle-class designers of these public baths also shaped working-class experiences of not only bathing, but of privacy as well.

Through the public bath movement, the middle class overtly targeted the working class and traditional bathing methods. Government officials, social activists, and leaders of industrial companies argued for the creation of public baths specifically for the poor and working class.[30] According to one public bath advocate, "baths [are] the most potent factor, after the public schools, in educating the poor towards a higher grade of citizenship."[31] Public bath proponents called for baths to be placed in the more populated areas of the city "occupied by the working classes and poorer people generally."[32] New York municipal officials adopted resolutions "emphasizing the immediate necessity for adequate bathing facilities in the tenement districts."[33] According to reformers, the public bath "must be as a temptation in the path of the tired workingman and the slum housewife."[34] One reformer called for public baths to be open all day on Sunday because "it seems inconsistent that a public bath, which is ostensibly maintained for the benefit of the laboring classes, should be closed on the particular day in which they are most at leisure to use it."[35] Public bath advocates proposed that these sites be completely free of charge or cost only a nominal amount.[36] Some public baths charged a small fee to furnish soap, towels, or bathing suits (for female patrons).[37] In contrast to the lavish and expensive private bathhouses, public baths were created to instill middle-class understandings of hygiene, cleanliness, and privacy in working-class patrons with few bathing alternatives.

Public bath proponents argued that members of the working class needed access to "proper" (that is, middle-class designed and regulated) bathing facilities for a variety of reasons. Middle-class reformers advocated for providing this access for moral, civic, and hygienic reasons. But because members of the working class could not afford dedicated bathrooms in their homes, their experience of privacy would be less exclusive. They were, after all, cleansing their bodies in "public" baths. While these spaces aligned with middle-class norms of gender segregation, the level of privacy bathers experienced clearly differed across class lines. This is reflected in the social construction of these sites.

Public bath designers and creators sought to construct spaces that would teach the working class how to bathe according to new middle-class standards. Public baths "had an educational value in encouraging the bathing habit" and gave members of the working class "an opportunity to learn how to be clean and . . . value health and decency in being physically clean," according to social commentators.[38] Public baths appear to have been an important component of efforts to improve the civic life of a community's working class. In urban areas such as Chicago, reformers argued that playgrounds and public baths were vital to improving the city's education system.[39] Public baths were also often placed in the same building as free libraries. In Albany, a settlement house in a largely immigrant neighborhood lent seventy-five thousand books per year through its free library and furnished up to eight hundred baths a day through its public bath.[40] When two northern Michigan mining companies built public libraries for their workers in the early 1900s, both companies decided to place public baths within the library buildings.[41] By placing public baths within these educational institutions, middle-class reformers evidently expected that the working class would also learn about personal cleanliness at these sites. For the creators of these spaces, imparting knowledge of hygiene was essential to enlightening and uplifting the working class.

Public bath proponents also employed the developing public health movement in their quest to reform the bathing experiences of members of the working class. As the germ theory came into prominence in the late nineteenth century, a public health movement focused on preventing disease in US cities through improvements in sewerage and water systems, as well as refuse collection.[42] Public health proponents also advocated personal cleanliness and hygiene.[43] As one reformer noted, "with the evolution of the germ theory of disease, the conviction has grown that the fundamental prophylaxis against all disease lies in hygienic habits and sanitary surroundings."[44] This commentary was specifically directed toward members of the working class, who needed access to "a generous supply of pure water [to] wash [disease] away beyond the possibility of doing any harm."[45] Since working-class housing usually lacked access to indoor plumbing, public baths were seen as an important component of the growing public health movement.

Public bath activists often tied public health with morality in their arguments for the establishment of public bathing facilities. As one social commentator noted, providing free public baths "will help to prevent typhoid, cholera, and crime . . . [and will] inspire sweeter manners and better observance of law."[46] Middle-class reformers specifically aimed their public bath movement efforts toward the working class, arguing that "public baths form one of the most effective and far-reaching of municipal institutions for the promotion of cleanliness, good health, and good citizenship."[47] These reformers believed that by simply cleansing the physical working-class body, "the moral, the social, and all other facilities" would necessarily be positively affected.[48]

Middle-class reformers clearly also hoped that public baths would address social issues. Working-class men with access to public baths would be in better health and would "think straight and live straight most of the time, at least."[49] Officials at one public bath decided to "furnish baths at beer prices," in the hopes of encouraging working-class men to spend five cents on a bath rather than a beer.[50] Middle-class reformers hoped that when working-class boys had access to sanctioned sites for exercise and hygiene, such as public gymnasiums and baths, they would be "little inclined to adopt questionable substitutes for these essential factors in the process of development into a worthy inhabitant of a republic."[51] In 1899, Boston mayor Josiah Quincy stated that the establishment of public baths (along with gymnasia and playgrounds) would result in "less disease, less intemperance, and, in the long run, less pauperism, crime, and insanity."[52] Middle-class public bath proponents framed this quest to control working-class behavior as part of their civic responsibility. As noted public bath proponent Simon Baruch argued, "it is the duty of a municipality to prevent disease, to prevent immorality ... [and] money spent for public baths [does] more toward raising the standard of health and morality than a much greater amount spent in any other way."[53]

Middle-class reformers argued that public baths offered members of the working class an alternative that they approved of and indeed wanted. The reformers cited impressive statistics about public bath patronage as an argument that members of the working class wanted access to bathing facilities. One public bath in New York recorded over seven hundred thousand baths a year and up to five thousand baths a day in the middle of summer (Figure 3.4).[54] Boston's public baths tallied nearly two million patrons in 1898 alone.[55] Public baths were also popular with industrial workers in more rural locations. The public bath in Calumet, Michigan, owned by the copper-mining company there, reported more than sixty thousand bathers in 1915, despite having a scattered, largely rural population of thirty thousand.[56] Public bath proponents highlighted statistics such as these as an argument for expanding the public bath movement and to show that the working class wanted access to bathing facilities. However, these middle-class reformers never asked whether public bath patrons would have preferred their own private bathrooms at home. Municipal officials, property owners, mining company executives, and industrial leaders (with the power to make these decisions) agreed

Figure 3.4. "Waiting for a Bath," from Bertha H. Smith, "The Public Bath," *The Outlook* 66, no. 2 (September 8, 1900): 566. Courtesy of Hathi Trust Digital Library.

that building large public bathhouses was a better solution than retrofitting existing working-class housing, largely because of cost.[57]

Public bath proponents also hoped to change the traditional bathing habits of newly arriving immigrants (often members of the working class). As one writer stated, "the greatest civilizing power that can be brought to bear on these uncivilized Europeans crowding into our cities lies in the public bath."[58] For middle-class reformers, the design, creation, and operation of public baths offered a means of instilling their values of hygiene and gender segregation in the growing working-class immigrant population. In 1882 alone, nearly eight hundred thousand people came to America. By 1907, the number of newly arriving immigrants rose to almost 1.3 million.[59] For example, New York City's population rose from nine hundred thousand in 1870 to 5.6 million in 1920, and foreign-born people accounted for 40 percent of the city's inhabitants throughout this time.[60] The "problem" was succinctly stated by one commentator at the time: "Since the Old World has been pouring its hordes of foreigners into this country, how can we civilize the lower classes of these people and make them good American citizens?"[61] The answer for many activists at the time was to offer these immigrants access to public bathing facilities: New York's first public bath was located in an Italian neighborhood, and soon "ninety-five percent in the waiting line [were] Italian."[62] According to one reformer, these Italians "gained self-respect, of which a clean white collar is an early symptom."[63] Access to daily bathing "had a very beneficial effect upon the foreign element, including all nationalities."[64] Social commentators connected public bath patronage with cleaner immigrant homes and an increased sense of self-worth.[65] Many of these immigrants were members of the larger American working class of the time. Underlying these arguments was the assumption that in order to "Americanize" the "foreign element," the middle-class values of personal hygiene and cleanliness needed to be instilled in them through the public bath.

The public bath movement was not initially overtly intended to change the working-class experience of privacy. Instead, contemporary commentators and social reformers (usually members of the middle class) advocated for bathing facilities for the working class on hygienic and moral grounds. Traditional methods of bathing were no longer considered hygienic according to middle-class standards. Rather than arguing for the provision of private bathrooms for the working class, reformers advocated for the creation of public baths. But bathing had become a highly exclusive, private act for the middle class. So that these new public baths could also be considered "private," middle-class creators designed the sites to be gender segregated. Public baths used gender exclusion as a means to shape the working-class experience of privacy in bathing.[66] As noted earlier, gender exclusion was not ensured in traditional home-bathing experiences. Thus emerging public baths were often the first spaces where members of the working class were exposed to this new understanding of privacy with respect to bathing.

By interrogating these spaces, we can begin to explore the limits of privacy, especially as it related to class. Public bath patrons experienced surveillance and external regulation while they engaged in the private act of bathing. This differed sharply from the total seclusion available to middle- and upper-class bathers in their private, domestic bathrooms.

While this newly emerging space could have taken on a variety of designs and forms, public baths were specifically created to physically express middle-class expectations of bodily privacy, as well as personal hygiene, sanitation, and even morality.[67] Privacy within the public baths was defined by gender and, at times, age exclusion. This privacy was also "classed," in that the working-class users' bathing experiences were highly monitored and controlled. This control was manifested through the presence of bath attendants and managers who often enforced bathing time restrictions, as well as the physical divisions built into public bath architecture. The working-class bathing experience thus emerged in stark contrast to the middle-class bathing traditions that were developing simultaneously. Just as middle-class homes gained a dedicated bathroom and running water, reformers and government officials decided that public bathhouses would be sufficient for cleansing the working class. While middle-class concerns over working-class morality, public health, class status, and gender segregation coalesced in initiating the public bath movement, the resulting physical spaces for public bathing created an experience of privacy deemed appropriate for the working class.

Designing Public Baths

Middle-class designers embedded their understandings and expectations of privacy into the public baths intended for the working class. These creators thus influenced the working-class experience of bodily privacy. The early public baths physically reflected some of the most essential components of a middle-class understanding of privacy. By exploring these physical sites as evidence, we can uncover middle-class values regarding privacy.

The public bathhouses proposed by reformers, engineers, municipal officials, and industrial leaders differed from the lavish private bathhouses available to urban middle- and upper-class Americans. Early public baths were often "floating baths" built on existing rivers and waterways. New York City's Department of Public Works built fifteen floating baths on the Hudson and East Rivers between 1870 and 1888. These baths were open only from June through September, but they furnished 2.5 million baths to males and 1.5 million to females each year. Bathers were allowed only twenty minutes to bathe, to prevent bathers (especially boys) from using the baths for recreation.[68] From the very beginning, these bathing spaces were regulated and monitored, in stark contrast to the private bathroom of the middle-class home.

As public baths became permanent edifices in cities and industrial communities across the United States, middle-class conceptions of privacy and hygiene became codified in structural form. The Calumet bath (mentioned above) offers an example of a typical early public bath. By exploring this bath, we can begin to answer questions prompted by these spaces. As described earlier, users, on entering the Calumet bath, were immediately separated by gender and age. Public bath users were separated by gender because of a shift in how the middle-class experienced privacy in regard to bathing. Having come to understand bathing as an exclusive act (in contrast to traditional bathing methods), middle-class designers tried to replicate this exclusion, albeit to a more limited degree, in newly created public baths.

Public bath designers used a number of material means to segregate men and women and afford them bodily privacy based on gender separation. Some public baths offered separate bathing facilities for men and women within the same building.[69] For one proposed bath in New York, "the plan has been drawn with a view of entirely separating males from females the moment they enter the building... not only for the bathers, but also for all employees.... No person in any part where there are females (whether bathers or employees) can go to any part where there are males, or vice versa, without passing through the central controlling-office on the main floor."[70] In another public bath, depicted in Figure 3.5, men and women were directed to separate entrances and waiting rooms. The men's facilities were twice as large, likely owing to men's greater use of public baths. The men's side also had a separate section for boys' baths, possibly due to a social norm that differentiated between boys' bodies and men's bodies. Girls, women, and likely small children were all grouped together in the women's side without concern for age.

Other public baths offered separate bath and shower rooms for men and women with a common pool (Figure 3.6). For these and other bathing facilities with common facilities for men and women, strict schedules of use

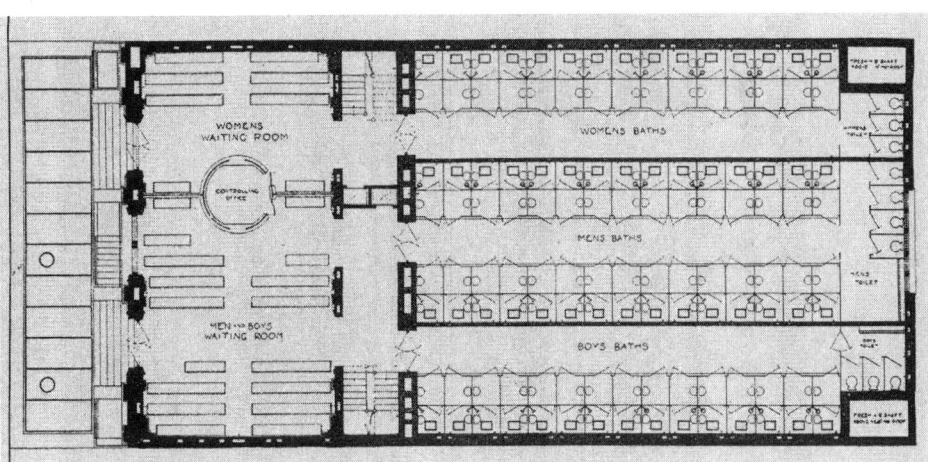

Figure 3.5. "Plan of Ground Floor," proposed public bath, from Mayor's Committee on Public Baths and Public Comfort Stations, *Report on Public Baths and Public Comfort Stations* (New York: Mayor's Committee, 1897), 182. Courtesy of Hathi Trust Digital Library.

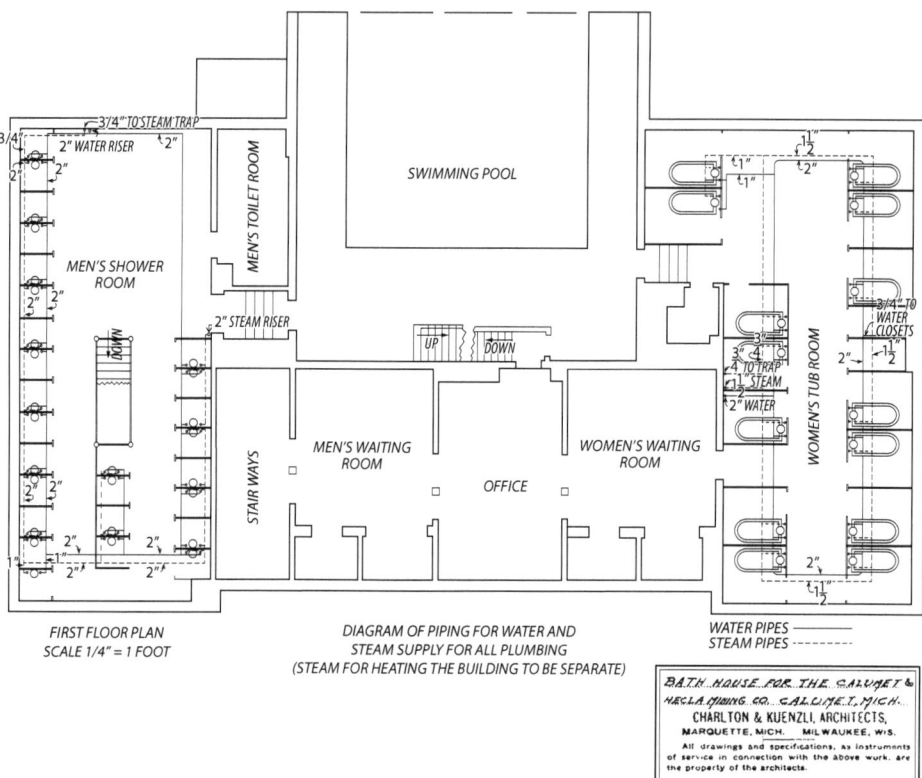

Figure 3.6. Based on "Bath House for the Calumet & Hecla Mining Co. Calumet, Mich.," 1911. C & H Drawings Collection, Michigan Technological University Archives and Copper Country Historical Collections. Redrawn by Jade Myers.

were created to segregate men and women. A 1914 schedule for the public baths in Manhattan indicates that men and women were admitted to the baths on alternating days from Monday to Saturday.[71] Other public baths had a much more complex schedule. At the Calumet public bath (Figure 3.6), patrons were allowed entrance at different times based on both gender and age. Men were permitted to use the baths and pool from 7 a.m. to 10 a.m. and noon to 4 p.m. on weekdays. Women and children used the baths and pool from 10 a.m. to noon on weekdays. The pool was open to boys from 4 p.m. to 6 p.m. on weekdays and 9 a.m. to noon on Saturdays. The rule book for the baths explicitly defined men as "males over 16," women as "females over 12," boys as "males between the ages of 10 and 16," and children as "males under 10 and females under 12."[72]

Male and female spaces in the newly emerging public baths were not only separate but also very different, underscoring the essentialness of gender distinction to middle-class expectations of bodily privacy. In addition to creating separate spaces or schedules for male and female bathers, many public baths offered a distinctly gendered experience for working-class bathers. At one bath, "the entrances for men and boys, that is, to the baths and the men's public comfort station, would be from the avenue" and thus more visible. The women's entrance gave them access to the baths, comfort station, and laundry and would be accessed "from the park side, the approaches so arranged as to be screened by shrubbery."[73] Public baths required women to wear bathing suits in bathing pools, even though most baths segregated male and female bathers.[74] Men and boys usually swam naked and were even encouraged to do so (Figure 3.7).[75] When Bruce Norden went to the Calumet public bath, "it was only the boys, not mixed. Of course you're stark naked, that's why."[76]

Many early public baths, including the Calumet public bath, offered tub and shower baths for men but only bathtubs for women. Most public baths in New York City followed suit, offering more showers for men than for women and more bathtubs for women than for men.[77] By the early twentieth century, many public bath proponents were advocating shower baths as more "sanitary" than tub baths.[78] Figure 3.8 shows an early shower bath in use (note that the patron in the photo is a boy, as an image of a naked female using a shower would have been highly inappropriate at the time). Reformers suggested locating these shower baths directly between dressing rooms and the bathhouse pool, for sanitary reasons, so that patrons would have no choice but to

Figure 3.7. "Calumet & Hecla Mining Company Swimming Pool in Bath House," 1913. Foster Collection, Library Card Photo #357, National Park Service, Keweenaw National Historical Park.

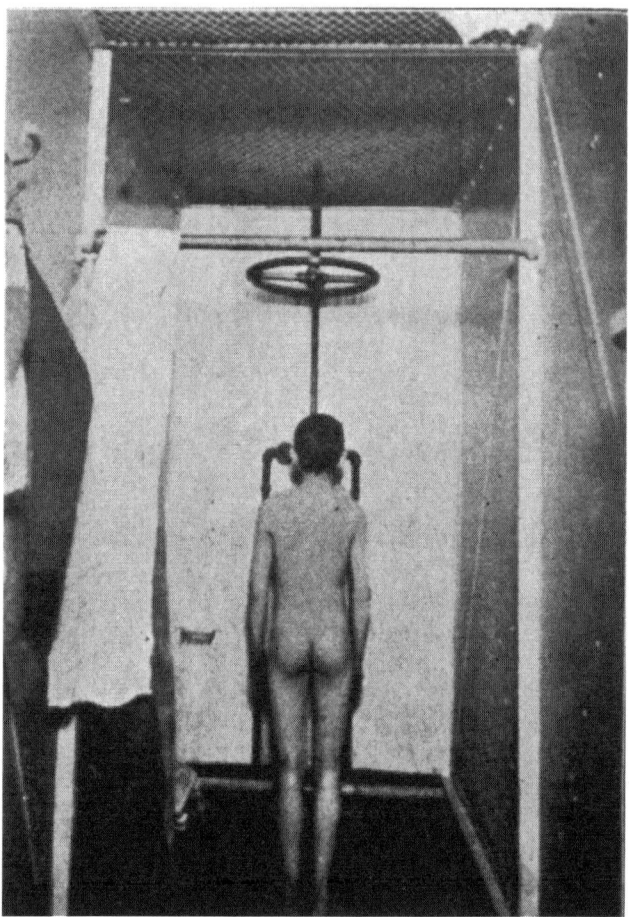

Figure 3.8. "The 'Ring,' one form of spray or shower bath, at the People's Bath," from Mayor's Committee on Public Baths and Public Comfort Stations, *Report on Public Baths and Public Comfort Stations* (New York: Mayor's Committee, 1897), 11. Courtesy of Hathi Trust Digital Library.

bathe before entering the common pool area.[79] In fact, the published rules for the public bath in Calumet, Michigan, stated that "no one will be allowed to use the swimming pool without first having taken a tub or shower bath."[80]

But the shower stall appears to have been initially gendered as a space offering privacy for male bodies. Although not stated outright in the literature of the time, the reason may be that women would have been able to keep their long hair dry by putting it up when taking a bath as opposed to when taking a shower. Figure 3.9 shows the interior of the men's shower

Figure 3.9. "Calumet & Hecla Showers in Bath House," MS003-25A-48-03829, Calumet & Hecla Photograph Collection, Michigan Technological University Archives and Copper Country Historical Collections.

room for the Calumet public bath. This room was equipped with twenty-eight shower baths. Although separated by dividers, the showers were open to the rest of the room. Figure 3.10 offers an interior view of the women's "tub rooms," which contained fourteen tubs.[81] Note the inclusion of individual doors to each of the women's tub rooms. Another public bath, created by the Quincy Mining Company in 1916, offered female bathers an outer room in each of the shower compartments "so that women if they wish can undress in the first compartment instead of the main room"[82] (Figure 3.11). These architectural arrangements, along with the rule allowing men and boys to swim naked, underscore the important middle-class gender distinctions that were reinforced by the public bath design and patrons' actual experience of these physical spaces. Clearly, women's bodies were treated very differently from male bodies; this contrast in body management influenced public bath designers and creators in defining these spaces as private.

Public Baths in Use

Public bath creators designed these spaces to offer bodily privacy to working-class bathers. Designers hoped working-class patrons would learn "proper"

Figure 3.10. "C & H Bath House, Bath Tubs and Toilets," MS003-009-014-01, Calumet & Hecla Photograph Collection, Michigan Technological University Archives and Copper Country Historical Collections.

bathing techniques through spatial interventions. One bath proponent noted the importance of placing restrooms "in the immediate vicinity of the cleansing baths . . . [with] large signs conspicuously posted, directing the bathers to use the toilet fixtures before going into the pool."[83] In order to keep the public baths sanitary, reformers suggested prohibiting patrons from spitting, smoking, chewing, or "urinating anywhere except in the toilets."[84] At every turn, working-class patrons were taught how to care for their bodies according to middle-class standards of hygiene and sanitation.

Medical experts also weighed in on how best to cleanse the working-class body. According to an article in *American Medicine*, preferred, "proper" bathing methods included "the tub-bath with pure water, possible only for the well-to-do and for a limited number in public bath-houses; . . . the spray or rain-bath, the sole method advisable in public baths."[85] The article railed against the popularity of the swimming pool because of how "impossible [it was] to keep the water pure if it is provided."[86] Physicians were also con-

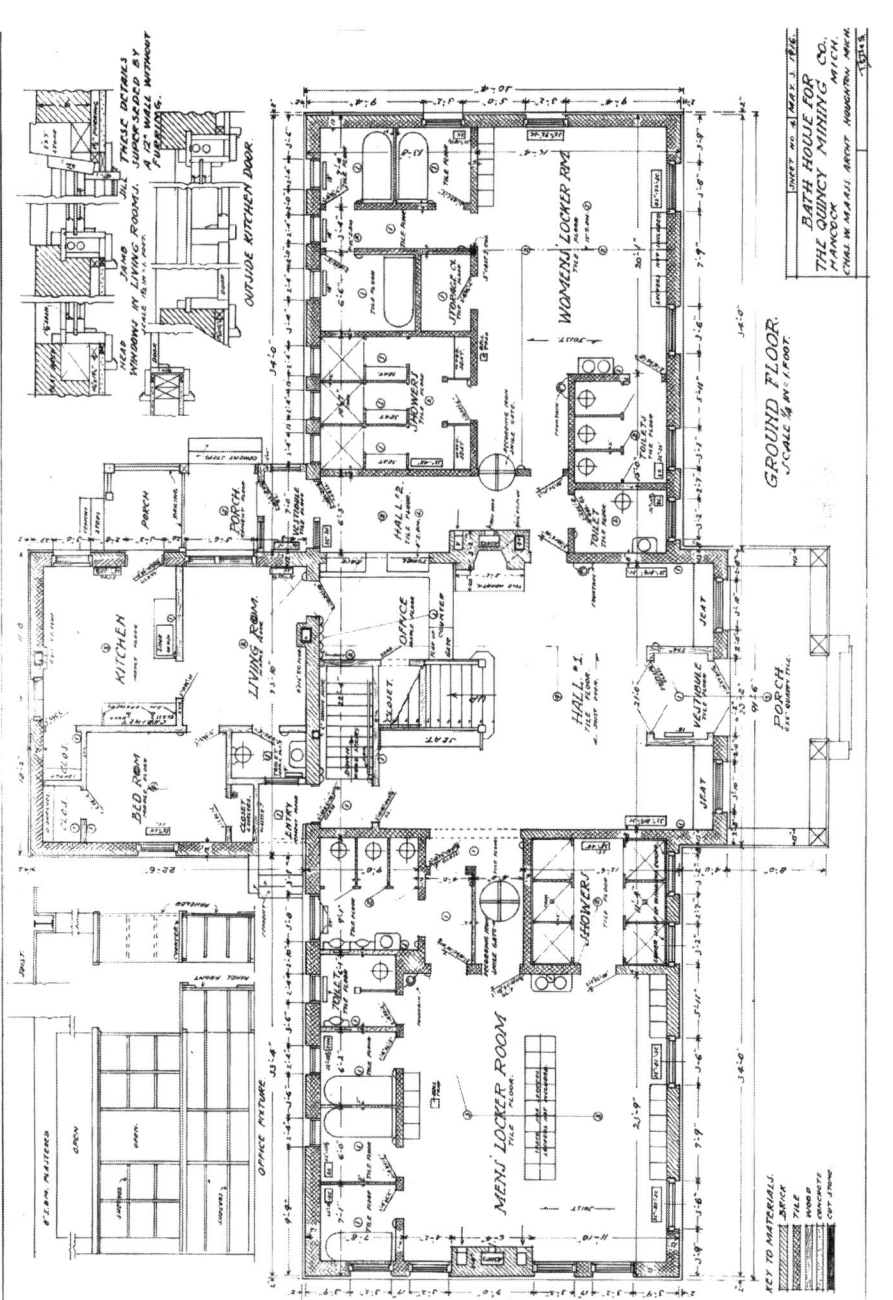

Figure 3.11. "Bath House for the Quincy Mining Co., Hancock, Mich.," ground floor plan, May 16, 1916, Historic American Engineering Record.

cerned that "unless the bathing is done unclothed, soap and cleanliness are not thought of, and even at best, modesty, that hardly-won virtue, is not encouraged in public bathing."[87] Underlying these sentiments was a concern over the cleanliness of the working-class body and how best to provide a hygienic environment for those bodies to be properly cleansed. According to contemporary physicians, public baths needed to offer working-class patrons clean running water, soap, and space for "modest" undressing.

Despite the fact that these gendered differences illustrated greater concern with women's bodily privacy, male patrons used public baths much more frequently than women. In 1895, 65,517 men and 12,580 women bathed at the People's Baths in New York.[88] At the Calumet bath, women accounted for 13 to 18 percent of patrons between 1912 and 1915.[89] Dean and Walter Cole, who remembered visiting their local public bath as boys, could not recall their mother ever going.[90] One contemporary commentator noted that although women's lack of enthusiasm for public baths was seen as evidence that women were not as "cleanly" as men, this assessment was "unjust."[91] The working-class woman, who usually served as "nurse, laundress, and seamstress" in her home, could not "walk the blocks between her home and the baths carrying one baby and followed by one or two more, and take a bath."[92] Patterns of use demonstrate that working-class women had difficulties getting away from their homes to use public baths or had misgivings about bathing in a public location.

Bathing under Surveillance

The public bath's physical design created bodily privacy for working-class patrons while manipulating the movement and experience of users throughout the space. These sites were also designed so that users could be watched and regulated by bath attendants, managers, and even police officers. These individuals created a level of surveillance not seen in middle-class private, home bathrooms. This important difference underscored that levels of bathing privacy varied according to a bather's class.

Working-class patrons were not alone when they entered the public baths, meaning that their experience of privacy further diverged from that of the middle class. Indeed, the most essential difference between the middle-class bathroom and the working-class public bath was whether or not bathers were allowed to be alone. Middle-class homeowners had paid for this ultimate control over their privacy, enabling them to exclude everyone but themselves. Because they could not afford their own dedicated bathrooms, public bath patrons had much less private bathing experiences than their middle-class counterparts. There were, of course, always other bath patrons present. But members of the working class were also surveilled by public bath managers and attendants. These individuals both assisted bathers and policed their behaviors, leading to a very different experience of privacy for the working-class public bath patron.

Although the physical spaces of these baths were meant to offer members of the working class privacy for cleansing their bodies, public bath owners often employed managers or attendants who controlled access to the baths. At the Calumet & Hecla bath, "the building [was] so arranged that all persons entering and leaving it [had to] pass through the [manager's] office."[93] The manager kept track of bathhouse attendance and collected fees.[94] Attendants often inspected bathers before entering the pool to make sure they had showered. As John Buckett recalled, when he bathed at the Calumet bath in the 1910s and 1920s, "they had somebody watching for the girls and somebody watching for the boys . . . [and] if you had dirty feet they weren't going to let you in the pool." His wife, Evelyn, remembered nuns making sure the girls had bathed before entering the pool.[95] Attendants were also on the lookout for unhealthy patrons. Bruce Norden recalled a time he did not pass inspection: "once I came out the shower, and I had a rash of sorts. [The attendant] was pointing, he looked over at me and he said 'out.'"[96] Managers and attendants, such as the man pictured in Figure 3.7, also monitored patron behavior. The manager at the Calumet & Hecla bath proposed allowing boys to use the bath for free "on account of the questionable ways some boys obtain money and coupons for towels."[97] The bath manager for the Quincy bath lived on-site, allowing for continual surveillance of bathhouse patrons and their activities. Under the watchful eyes of these managers and attendants, working-class patrons experienced a class-based privacy within these public baths.

Some public baths did not even allow users to control the length or temperature of their baths. Chicago's first free public bath was opened in 1894 in "one of the most thickly populated centers of Chicago's working classes."[98] A bath attendant regulated the temperature of the water via a large mixing table outside of the shower and bath stalls. The same attendant timed the hot water to be available for 8 minutes, the cold water to be available for 2 minutes, and the bather to have 10 minutes total to undress and dress.[99] Bathers were advised when they needed to begin their "final rinse-off." Attendants echoed posted signs stating that bathers had 15 minutes for dressing after their bath.[100] Similarly, the People's Bath in New York allowed bathers 20 minutes, "ample time for a bath."[101] The regulated and standardized experiences of these patrons severely limited their sense of autonomy and control over how they cleansed their bodies.

Yet petty crimes such as theft still occurred at public baths.[102] Some public baths went to great lengths to protect patrons as well as monitor their behavior. The office to one bath in New York was situated so that "one person can control both of the main entrances (male and female), and all of the entrances to the various baths, staircases, etc. . . . [and] no one can enter or leave the building without being seen from here, excepting, of course, those using the public comfort stations and public laundry."[103] Several other baths had regular police presence. The People's Bath in New York boasted that "the police authorities have kindly detailed an officer as a regular attendant, and perfect order is maintained."[104] At a Chicago public bath, "Police Officer Whitney" was commended for "his perfect control of those attending."[105] This level of regulation and control certainly aided in maintaining the gender exclusion deemed necessary to afford privacy to working-class bathers, but it is doubtful that many middle-class Americans had to pass a police officer on their way to take a bath.

⁓

While the middle class began to increasingly bathe in plumbed, private bathrooms within their own homes, working-class Americans continued to bathe via more traditional means, due to their lack of indoor plumbing and bathrooms. Middle-class proponents of public baths wanted to offer access to bathing facilities to working-class Americans while instilling a middle-class understanding of bodily privacy (as well as cleanliness, hygiene, and morality) and while improving overall public health. These public baths were gender segregated, aligning them with a foundational component of emerging middle-class expectations regarding privacy. But these were still *public* baths and diverged from the private, domestic bathrooms enjoyed by most upper- and middle-class Americans at this time. The privacy offered in these public baths was tempered by bath managers and attendants who policed bath activities while inspecting patrons' physical health and hygiene. Gender exclusion was of the utmost importance to the designers and creators of these public baths, but the privacy offered within these spaces was class-based and differed from the domestic bathing sites that had become fixtures in the middle-class home.

CHAPTER FOUR

Creating Privacy in Public

Public Comfort Stations

In 1897, the New York City Mayor's Committee on Public Baths and Public Comfort Stations recommended that the city build public toilet facilities based on the example of London's underground latrines, because they were "clean, inodorous, hidden from view, attractive, frequented by all ranks of society, and . . . provided for both men and women in separate places" (Figure 4.1).[1]

Fifteen years later, the quest for ideal public toilet facilities continued as the *Engineering Review* extolled the exemplary design of a "public comfort station," as it was termed at the time, in Brookline, Massachusetts. This comfort station was "ideally" located at the convergence of several streetcar lines in the most densely populated area of the city. The *Review* made specific note of the facility's separate entrances for men and women "designed with covered vestibules and right angle turns in the staircases, thus securing the maximum of privacy."[2] Once inside, women could have used one of the individual toilet stalls and washed their hands at a sink in the common outer room. Women also had the option of entering a "retiring room." Men chose from individual stalls or urinals. They were not offered a retiring room (Figure 4.2).

These assessments of early public toilets highlight how privacy was defined at a time when Americans were increasingly spending time in public away from their private homes. Public comfort stations needed to offer privacy for potential users to consent to the private act of relieving themselves within these new public sites. Creators and designers (who were usually members of the middle class) defined these spaces as private by physically and visually segregating the spaces (and stalls within the sites) from public areas around the comfort station. Creators also divided and excluded users based on gender, race, and class distinctions. Together, the spatial and social construction of these spaces afforded users explicit privacy in public.

Figure 4.1. "Underground Lavatory (Interior), Charing Cross, London," from Mayor's Committee on Public Baths and Public Comfort Stations, *Report on Public Baths and Public Comfort Stations* (New York: Mayor's Committee, 1897): 156. Courtesy of Hathi Trust Digital Library.

Through this spatial case study, we can investigate how creators grappled with multiple dimensions of privacy at the same time in their design of public toilet facilities for a variety of users. These spaces were designed to incorporate different conceptions of privacy depending on the different users the spaces were likely to encounter. Gender separation remained a consistent element of privacy, whereas race and class were treated differently in the design of the space depending on the circumstances of the designer and the user. For example, explicit racial separation predominated in the design of restrooms in the American South, but not in the North. Other site designs made it possible for members of the upper to middle classes to pay a fee to have more elements of privacy than working-class users.

But while these sites offered privacy to users, comfort stations were also available to the general public. The inherently public aspect of these spaces also left them vulnerable to misuse and transgressions. Creators and designers of these sites installed comfort station attendants and managers (even po-

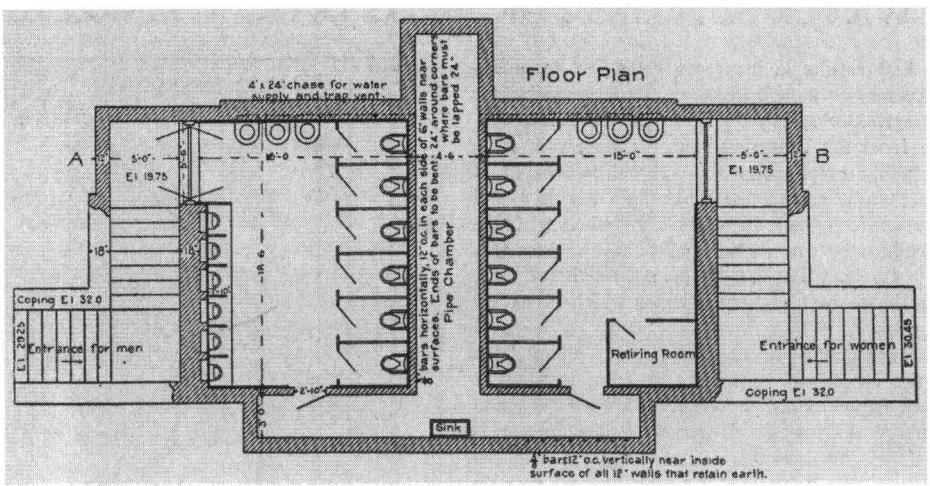

Figure 4.2. "Public Comfort Station at Brookline, Mass.," from "The Public Comfort Station in America," *Engineering Review* 22, no. 5 (May 1912): 37. Courtesy of Science, Industry & Business Library, The New York Public Library.

lice officers) to regulate and maintain these sites. While these newly emerging spaces clearly filled a void in the growing public landscape of the early twentieth century, the prescriptive definition of privacy implemented by social commentators and comfort station designers was often at odds with the actual experience of these stations by patrons. In this spatial case study, we find a space where users pushed back against physical and social constraints.

Few Options for Relief

The need for public toilet facilities was stated succinctly by a doctor of the time: "There is no need to insist upon or to emphasize the annoyance, the humiliating experiences and the dangers to health caused to the shopping and traveling public by this barbarous absence of modern sanitary conveniences."[3] Prior to the push for the widespread creation of distinct public toilet facilities in the 1890s to 1930s, other sites often served Americans' need for relief. Saloons and hotels offered public toilets, but these facilities were usually reserved for paying customers. As one commentator noted, "most cities are well supplied with hotels, restaurants and *saloons* [sic], which men, women, girls and boys are too often forced to make use of because of the absence of necessary public comfort stations."[4] This reliance on saloons for public relief proved especially problematic for social commentators at the turn of the century, who stated that "the provision of public comfort stations may lead to the discouraging of the glass, taken often when not greatly desired, to recompense the saloon keeper."[5] At a dance hall in Chicago, the toilet facilities for men were "reached only by going through the bar and there [was] an unwritten code that the man who avails himself of the privilege must spend money for a drink."[6] The closure of saloons with the onset of Prohibition in 1920 further limited the public's options for toilet facilities.[7] Larger businesses, such as banks, also offered "toilet-rooms," but only for banking patrons, who were more likely to be members of the middle and upper classes. As department stores developed in the late nineteenth century, they offered another public toilet site, albeit one reserved for store customers. Women especially availed themselves of department store toilets, as women's presence in saloons was not socially acceptable at the time.[8] One public comfort station proponent noted that "even in the days before prohibition women were seriously penalized [as] few women, especially those with young children, were willing to enter a saloon for the purpose of obtaining relief."[9]

But none of these spaces was truly public. Without any option for public relief, many had to make do with alternative sites that were not suited to this purpose. Social commentators at the time were concerned that, without public toilet facilities, some members of the working class were reduced to "committing nuisances in alleys and slightly out of the way corners."[10] Nineteenth-century physicians in urban areas were concerned that their patients were all too often forced to "skip . . . into a chance stable or boardyard, or sneak up a dark alley at imminent risk of being confronted by stray passers, or the worse choice of going into a vile dram-shop in order to find a place to relieve an all too full bladder."[11] Neighborhood boys in urban areas were known to "commit all manner of nuisances" in vacant city lots.[12] The problem was so widespread that contemporary medical experts noted that "the passer-by on our most public thoroughfares is constantly . . . reminded of the fact that urine . . . undergoes rapid decomposition on exposure to air, emitting a most offensive and sickening odor."[13] While these practices certainly resulted in "bad odors," middle-class reformers were most concerned that "such places were in view of the passing public, whose sensibilities [were] disgusted or shocked."[14]

Gendered Options for Relief

Some early efforts at providing public relief were targeted specifically at men who frequently availed themselves of alleyways, as evidenced by "stained walls" and the frequent posting of "Commit No Nuisance" signs.[15] Early public urinals consisted of simple metal walls with no entrance doors (Figure 4.3). Men would enter through an opening in the walls, turn a corner, and find a urinal attached to the wall of an open alcove. Such a setup allowed for awkward encounters and intrusions of personal space when urinals were in use as incoming users turned the corner.

But a push for public urinals in the late nineteenth century left few options for women to find relief in public.[16] While sources on female alternatives for "public comfort" are scarce, historian Barbara Penner has uncovered several ways British women dealt with relieving themselves in public during this time. Some women limited their time away from home so they could return if the need arose.[17] Upper-class women who owned private carriages had the option of carrying a portable chamber pot for use in their travels around the city.[18] Women of more modest means were reduced to the same alleys and out-of-the-way corners as their male counterparts, with only their long skirts for coverage.[19] The options for American women were likely very similar. The

Figure 4.3. "Mott's Sectional Street or Park Urinals," Plate 606-G, "Three Person Urinal with Two Entrances" from *Catalogue "G": Illustrating the Plumbing and Sanitary Department of the J. L. Mott Iron Works* (New York: J. L. Mott Iron Works, 1888), 241. Courtesy of Science, Industry & Business Library: General Collection, The New York Public Library. New York Public Library Digital Collections. Accessed June 24, 2020. http://digitalcollections.nypl.org/items/510d47db-ce97-a3d9-e040-e00a18064a99.

difficulty of finding public toilet facilities likely prevented women from leaving their homes to venture out in public as often as they might have. The widespread need for sanitary public conveniences was acute, but most especially for working-class women.

The creation of public restrooms was precipitated by a series of societal shifts at the turn of the twentieth century. Dramatic population increases, spurred by increasing immigration, led to a sharp increase in urbanization. New urban spaces, including department stores and other sites of consumption, increasingly called people out of their homes and into public spaces. More people in new public spaces led to a need for new sites of relief.

Proponents of public comfort stations made their case on sanitary, hygienic, and moral grounds. Public comfort stations were defined as "public buildings or structures intended to afford toilet conveniences for either one or else for both sexes . . . [with] complete installation of water-closets, urinals, lavatories, drinking fountains and other toilet accessories, also rest rooms" (Figure 4.4).[20] By 1915, one public official noted that the severe lack of such facilities was "the most flagrant failure in American sanitation today."[21] Although the earliest New York City comfort stations dated from the late nineteenth century, there were only sixty-five designated public comfort stations throughout the entire five boroughs by 1930 (aside from those located in parks). This number was "totally inadequate," according to social reformers of the time.[22] Not only was an adequate number of stations required to maintain sanitary conditions, comfort stations also needed to be well situated and well maintained to discourage "riff-raff . . . [who] bring the filthy habits of their lives," according to one commentator.[23] And by offering pay stalls, newspaper stands, and telephone and information booths, public comfort stations could be self-sustaining and affordable for any community.[24] According to social commentators, sanitary, convenient comfort stations would be morally uplifting without creating undue expense to the community.

Public restrooms were designed to afford physical and visual separation between users and also between them and nonusers. Public restrooms were also designed to segregate various social groups who would potentially use the space. Men and women were universally separated in restrooms, as evidenced by the physical spaces themselves. At times, designers created differing experiences of privacy for users of different socioeconomic classes. Finally, while northern examples of public restrooms implicitly imposed separation by race, Southern examples created explicitly racially segregated physical spaces.

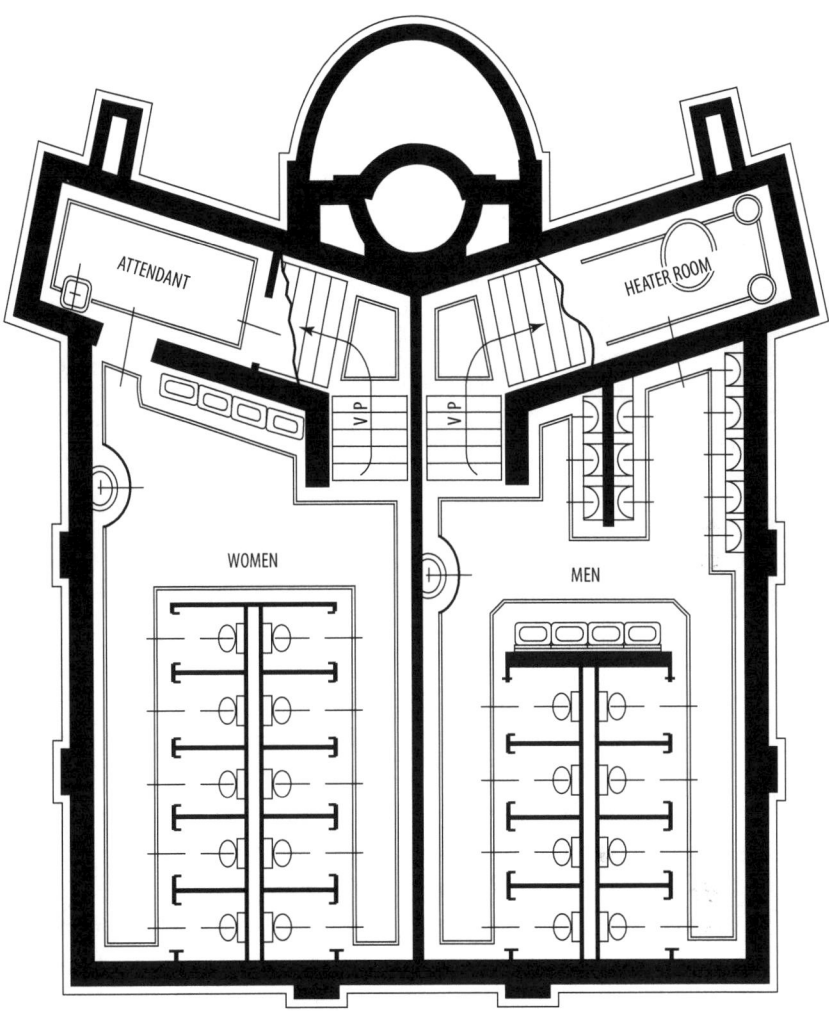

Figure 4.4. Based on Van Leyen, Schilling, and Keogh, "Public Comfort Station, Capital Square, Detroit, Mich.," *American Architect* 118, no. 2342 (November 10, 1920): 610. Redrawn by Jade Myers.

Physical Construction: Visual and Aural

Public comfort stations were sites at the boundary of the public and private. In reexamining the *Engineering Review*'s praise for an exemplary early public comfort station, we can begin to see how an ideal privacy could be physically created within one of these sites. One of the most essential ways privacy was physically created in public-private spaces was visually (Figure 4.5). The *Review* commended the Brookline comfort station's underground location

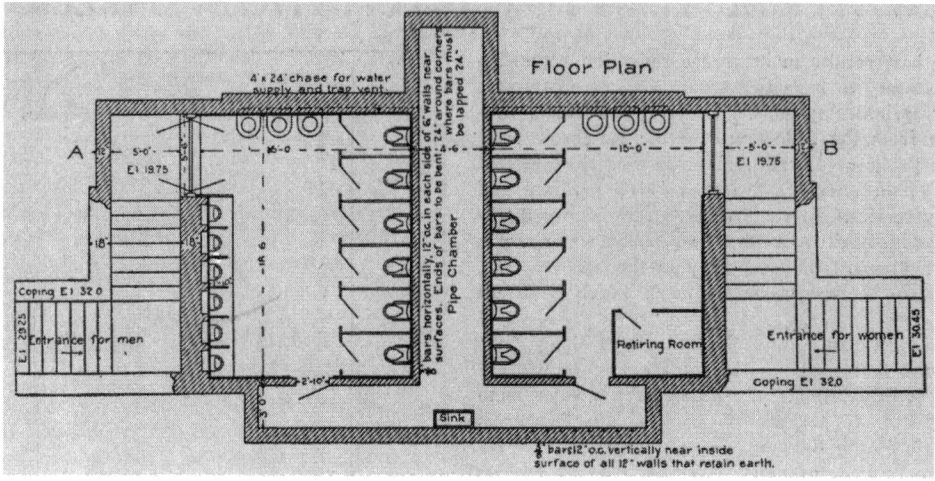

Figure 4.5. "Public Comfort Station at Brookline, Mass.," from "The Public Comfort Station in America," *Engineering Review* 22, no. 5 (May 1912): 37. Courtesy of Science, Industry & Business Library, The New York Public Library.

and hidden entrances. Patrons would have entered the station from the street, descending separate staircases for men and women. At the bottom of the stairs, users would have passed through an entrance hidden from the view of the passing public. Once inside, users would have been visually protected from other patrons by partitions at urinals or stall walls and doors. Designs for public comfort stations highlight the use of individual stalls and walls as visual barriers for patrons. The stalls needed to have doors "large enough to afford privacy" (Figure 4.6).[25] These internal visual barriers had their limits. Comfort station users were still forced to encounter other patrons in the common areas of the room, as these were public spaces. Stall doors did not extend to the floors, allowing patrons to know which stalls were in use by looking for feet under the door. Mirrors lining the walls above the sink would have encouraged users to look up and see who else was in the room as they washed their hands. Still, the private act of relieving oneself was, at least partly, visually protected.

Many social commentators were proponents of locating public comfort stations underground, in order to visually separate the entire building from the public sites in which they were situated (Figure 4.7).[26] While underground comfort stations were preferred to completely protect toilet facilities from public view, one engineer noted that plants could shield the entrance of a comfort station "without being so very conspicuous."[27] Other propo-

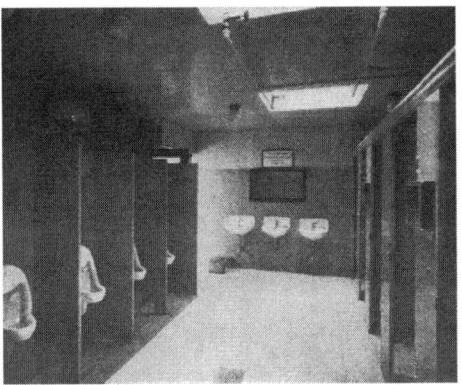 

Figure 4.6. Men's toilet (left) and women's toilet (right) in public comfort station, Brookline, Massachusetts, from "The Public Comfort Station in America," *Engineering Review* 22, no. 5 (May 1912): 36. Courtesy of Science, Industry & Business Library, The New York Public Library.

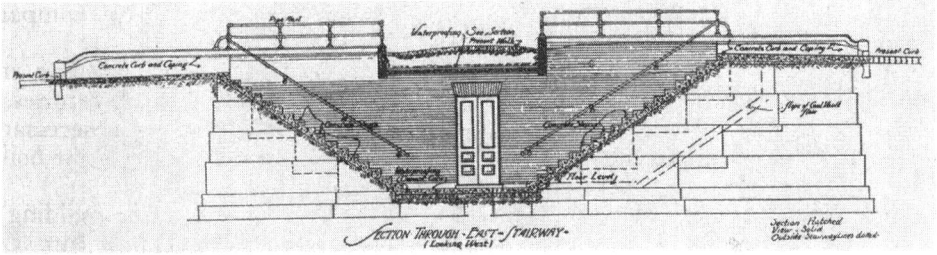

Figure 4.7. "Public Comfort Station No. 2, District of Columbia," from "Planning Public Comfort Stations," *Sanitary Pottery* 6, no. 12 (April 1915): 13. Courtesy of Science, Industry & Business Library, The New York Public Library.

nents argued that a public comfort station building should "not be too conspicuous but should be an architectural gem, harmonizing with the surroundings."[28] Another commentator was more succinct, stating public comfort stations needed to be "made ornate and attractive, rather than ugly and repellant."[29] It was important that it was not obvious from looking at the comfort station what went on inside.

This preoccupation with visual privacy stood in stark contrast to some European precedents for public relief. While one commentator noted an abundance of public toilet facilities in Europe, "not all are as completely equipped as those found in America."[30] In some cities, especially Paris, urinals were placed in public areas with a small screen to create a minimum amount of visual privacy (Figure 4.8). However, these screens did nothing to disguise the activities that were going on behind them. As one American public comfort station proponent noted, "not merely is their publicity disgusting, but they are fully objectionable on the ground of uncleanliness."[31] Another commentator stated that the public urinals in Paris were inappropriate for "adoption in the country [because] the location of many is too conspicuous."[32] London, however, "boast[ed] many fine comfort stations, chiefly located underground" (including the example at the beginning of the chapter).[33] Visual privacy inside and outside public comfort stations was an essential part of their acceptability as private spaces.

And while comfort station designers attempted to offer users as much visual privacy as possible, sounds and smells would have been an inexorable part of the actual experience. Whether sounds were coming from fellow patrons or from the comfort station equipment, it would have been difficult for users to feel as though they were in a completely private space. One con-

Figure 4.8. Charles Marville, "Urinoir système Jennings, Plateau de l'Ambigu," c. 1865. *Vespasienne* (public urinal) on the Grands Boulevards, Paris. Courtesy of The State Library of Victoria. Gift, Government of France, 1881.

temporary toilet manufacturer advertised a "silent" toilet so that users would not be "embarrassed by noise escaping from the bath or toilet-room when the closet is flushed."[34] Regardless of how clean and sanitary these spaces were intended to be, their essential function was for human waste elimination. The accompanying smells and sounds would have been impossible to completely mitigate.

Social Construction: Gender Separation

Gender separation was an essential social component of a middle-class understanding of privacy that was clearly built into the physical spaces of early restrooms. As the *Engineering Review* noted, "maximum privacy" could be achieved only through the total separation of men and women. The Worcester, Massachusetts, comfort station shown in Figure 4.9 offers an example of how gender segregation was achieved. The male and female entrances were located diagonally across from one another so that men and women would not need to encounter one another as they entered their separate sections of the station. From their separate entrances, men and women would enter two very different comfort station rooms. The men's side contained urinals as well as stalls, while the women's side contained only stalls. Since the station's janitor or maintenance worker was more than likely male, access to the station's plumbing and heating areas was located on the men's side of the station. This left less room for sinks and mirrors on the men's side, and thus the men's washing and grooming fixtures were much smaller and less elaborate than on the women's side. In addition, women had the option of resting in their female-only retiring room or on a large marble seat outside the retiring room, while men were left with no other option than to leave once they had relieved themselves. Thus women and men were not only segregated in public comfort stations but also had a very gendered experience of these stations. This suggests that middle-class designers believed that the needs of men's and women's bodies differed when performing the act of relieving themselves.

It was also customary for men and women to have entirely separate entrances to facilities in the same building, to ensure immediate separation on entry to these spaces. These entrances were often located as far away from each other as possible.[35] For example, the State Board of Health of Wisconsin was tasked with providing state-mandated public comfort stations with "suitable approaches and privacy, separating accommodations afforded both

74 Private Spaces in Public Places

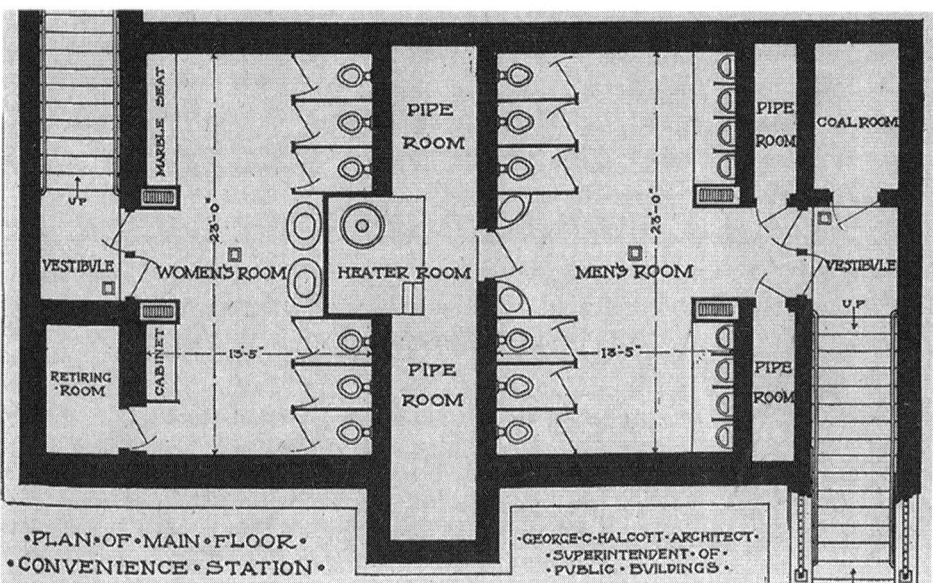

Figure 4.9. "Public Comfort Station, Worcester, Mass." from "The Public Comfort Station in America," *Engineering Review* 22, no. 8 (August 1912): 37. Courtesy of Science, Industry & Business Library, The New York Public Library.

sexes."[36] Other stations were housed in completely separate buildings for male and female users. The assumption of gendered separation helped to create a sense of privacy within these spaces.

It appears that, for at least some women, it nevertheless took some time before the privacy offered in newly created public comfort stations was considered acceptable. Early estimates of comfort station users showed that only 15 to 20 percent were women.[37] There was also a corresponding reluctance by women to patronize public baths during this time (see Chapter 3). One doctor at the time argued that women had a "false modesty or squeamishness about being seen going to the toilet while in public places."[38] This difference in use was likely informed by societal norms concerning the female body, as contemporary commentators noted there "would naturally be expected a greater delicacy and reluctance on the part of women" in using public comfort stations.[39] Another reason for the discrepancy in use could stem from the fact that men had a longer-established custom of public relief, either through the use of early public urinals or saloon toilets or through simply standing partly hidden in an alleyway. The social norm of gendered segregation of private activities shaped the built environment of these private spaces in public. And female and male bodies experienced these spaces differently, largely due to their gender.

Some comfort stations offered differing amenities for men and women. Women's comfort stations often included rooms for resting or retiring, while the men's side rarely, if ever, had such rooms (Figure 4.10). Other stations offered "emergency rooms" on the women's side where women could lie down on a cot while "medical attendance" was summoned on one of the provided telephones.

Female attendants also sold sanitary napkins and combs, and provided sewing notions and clothes brushes for female patrons.[40] Other stations offered accommodations for women with children (Figure 4.11). Such distinctions highlight a very different understanding of the needs of men and women. In addition to requiring facilities for relief in public, female patrons were thought to need special areas for rest and possible medical intervention. Men simply needed a place to "go" and nothing more. Middle-class designers created spaces where men and women were strictly separated, and their bodies were interpreted and treated unequally.

Social Construction: Classing Privacy

Early public restrooms also offer evidence about how middle-class designers, government officials, and businesses considered privacy in relation to class. For the creators of these sites, class distinctions were often implemented in the physical experience of these spaces. Although it is difficult to ascertain precisely who used these early comfort stations, they were at least built with the intent to serve "all classes."[41] One proponent listed potential users as "women shoppers and visitors, frequently accompanied by little children, transient travelers without hotel accommodation, working men and women,

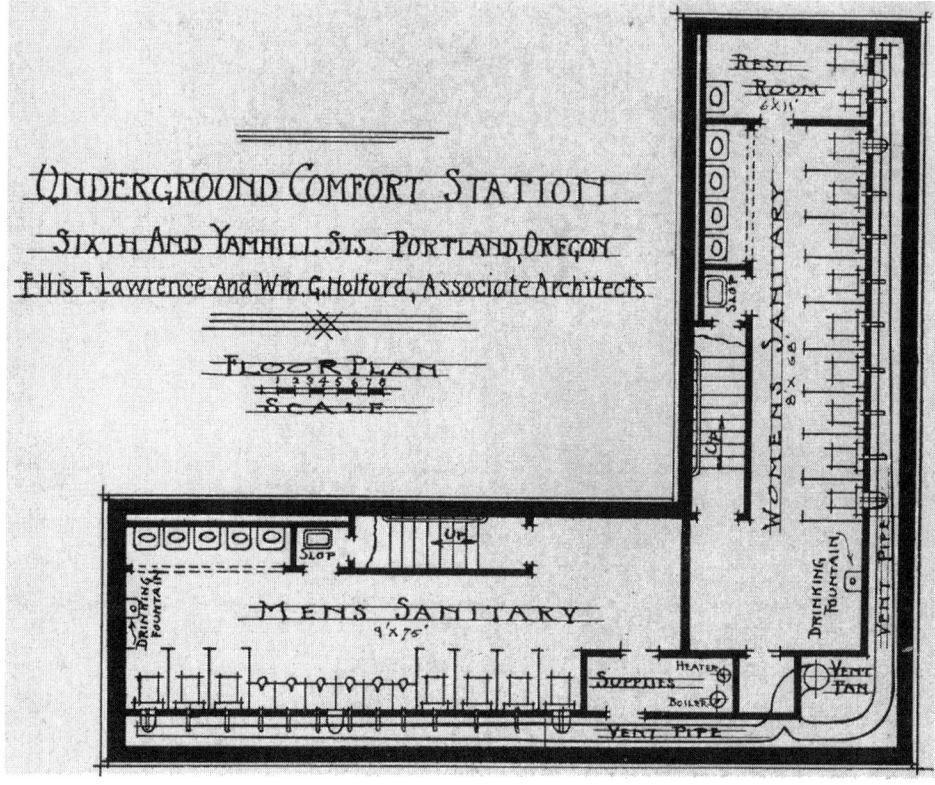

Figure 4.10. "Underground Comfort Station," from "Public Comfort Stations in Portland, Ore.," *Sanitary Pottery* 6, no. 5 (September 1914): 13. Courtesy of Science, Industry & Business Library, The New York Public Library.

postmen, street employees, newsboys, messengers . . . school children, the aged, and the unemployed seeking work."[42] Although "women shoppers" could have included middle-class women, members of the middle and upper classes did have alternatives to comfort stations in the businesses they patronized, including banks and department stores.

Middle-class designers at times constricted the use of early public restrooms by class. Some facilities required customers to pay to use them. At other sites, users could pay for greater exclusion within these spaces, creating a class-based experience of privacy (Figure 4.11). In the comfort station pictured in Figure 4.12, paying users could access separate sinks and toilets from nonpaying station users. These toilets and sinks were located in completely separate areas of the station. While nonpaying users had to wash their hands in sinks in an "ante room," users who were willing or able to pay could

Figure 4.11. Fredrick L. Ford, "Detroit, Mich. Pay compartment for mother and child," from "Monograph on Public Comfort Stations," in *Fourth Annual Report of the Commission on the City Plan to the Mayor and Court of Common Council, City of Hartford, Connecticut* (Hartford: Hartford Press, 1911), 28. Courtesy of Hathi Trust Digital Library.

wash their hands in the more private area of the pay toilet room. Other comfort stations offered differing levels of comfort and privacy for paying customers. Social commentators recommended turnstiles to divide free and pay portions in public comfort stations so that "those paying... will have use of the greater space as well as the toilet booth."[43] Patrons of another comfort station could gain access to more privacy for a price. After paying a small fee and passing through a turnstile, men and women could access a portion of the station with more sinks or, as on the women's side, private sinks within each stall. These pay sides were also served by a maid and porter, suggesting that the pay area would have been cleaner and more accommodating than the free side.

Inside individual pay stalls or compartments, the amenities continued to improve for those who could afford them. The pay compartments in the comfort station in Figure 4.12 were large enough to allow "hot and dirty travelers

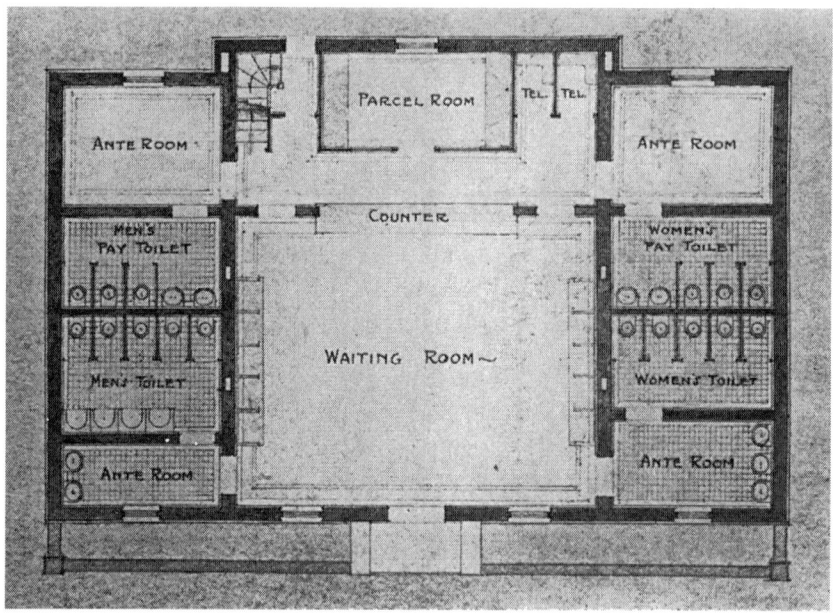

Figure 4.12. "Floor Plan of National Highways Public Comfort Station," from "The Comfort Station as a Public Utility," *American City* 16, no. 2 (February 1917): 180. Courtesy of the University of Delaware Library.

to take a refreshing sponge bath."[44] Some pay closets were equipped with door locks, while the free stalls had simple bolts.[45] In addition to purchasing "greater privacy," comfort station users could pay for "greater cleanliness and a higher grade of fixtures."[46] In some cases, the pay stalls had doors, while the free toilets of the comfort station did not.[47] Most pay compartments had individual sinks and towels, "secur[ing] the user entire privacy."[48] According to one trade journal, the cost for "entire privacy" was one to five cents per use.[49] The disparities of access and aesthetics based on price served to "class" these spaces and the level of privacy experienced within them, thus materializing the social distinctions of class during this time.

Social Construction: Racial Segregation

Public restrooms also reflected middle-class society's perceptions regarding race. Although not always overtly stated or clearly physically manifested, there was always at least an implied assumption that public toilet facilities would be racially segregated. The idea of creating separate, racialized areas was at least novel enough to a national audience to merit an article in the *American Architect* in 1922. In the article, titled "Dallas Public Comfort Station: A Comfort Station in Which Provisions Are Made for Two Races," the author noted that "public comfort stations in Northern cities, where the race question is not raised, are simple by comparison to similar utilities in the South" (Figure 4.13).[50] According to the article, the city of Dallas answered the "race question" by creating "four separate divisions" within the facility. Although it was "desirable to have separate stairways for the two races, space did not permit," according to the article. The comfort station therefore offered only two separate stairways and entrances for men and women, which led patrons to different sections according to race. Of

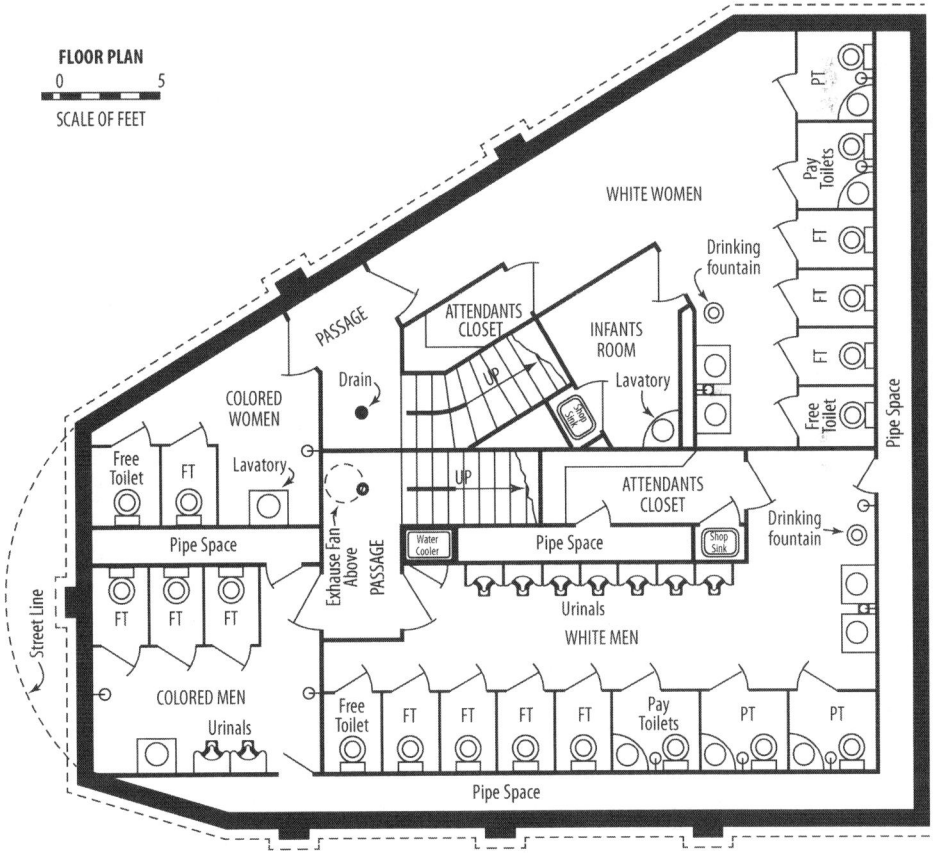

Figure 4.13. Based on "Dallas Public Comfort Station: A Comfort Station in Which Provisions Are Made for Two Races," *American Architect and the Architectural Review* 121, no. 2389 (May 15, 1922): 232. Redrawn by Jade Myers.

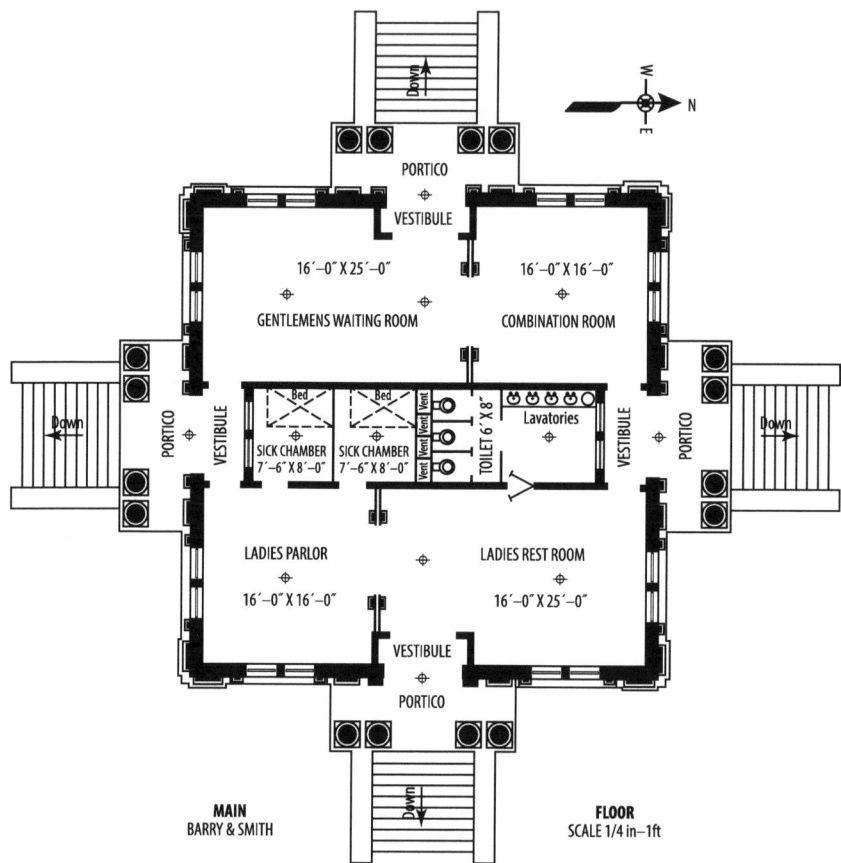

Figure 4.14. Based on "Paris, Texas, Is to Build a Magnificent Public-Comfort Station Early Next Year," *Domestic Engineering* 57, no. 4 (October 28, 1911): 86–87. Redrawn by Jade Myers.

more concern to the article's author was the fact that the male and female entrances were too "close together." But a large evergreen plant was placed between the two entrances, and "no complaints ha[d] been made."[51] An earlier comfort station located in Paris, Texas, did offer racially and gender-segregated entrances, but the accompanying article did not make mention of these divisions (Figure 4.14).[52] The racially segregated sides of the comfort station in Figure 4.13 were separate and clearly unequal. The "white women's" side was not only much larger than the "colored women's," but white women were also afforded a designated attendant and separate "infant room." In addition, the areas designated for "white women" and "white men" contained

Creating Privacy in Public 81

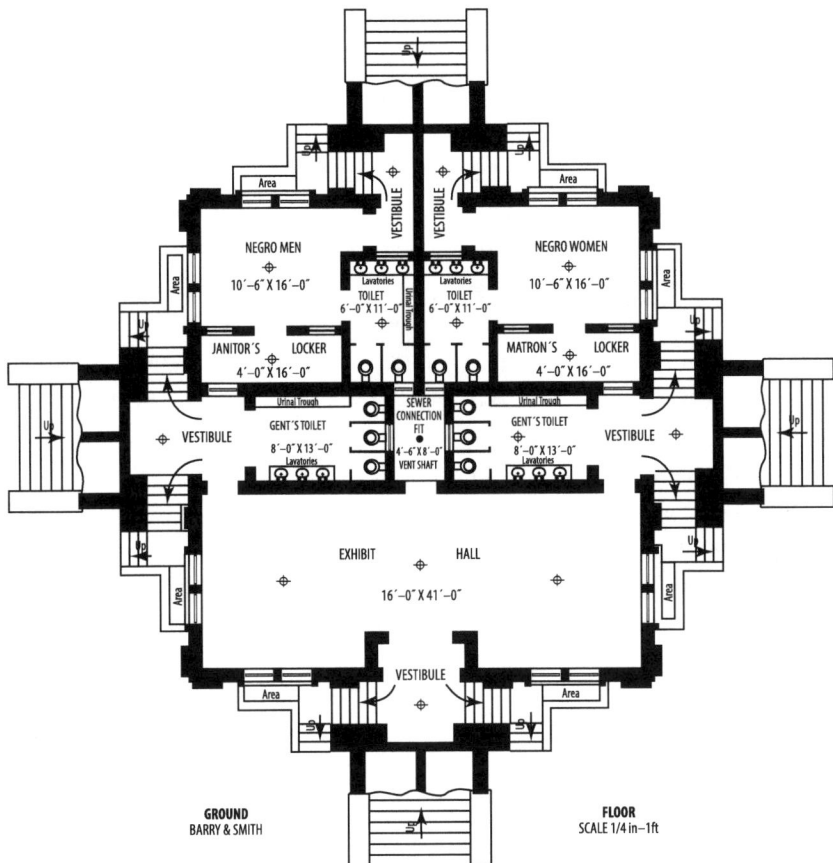

Figure 4.14. (continued)

both "free toilets" and "pay toilets," the area designated for "colored women" and "colored men" had no option other than "free toilets." Whether overtly physically manifested or simply implied, this definition of privacy was also based on racial segregation.

Here we can see middle-class designers' perceptions of race physically manifested. These examples underscore race as another category of social exclusion used to define comfort stations' privacy. It appears that northern and southern comfort station designers enforced this exclusion. Most contemporary periodicals were published in northern cities, and thus discuss northern sites much more often. From these examples, we can surmise that racial exclusion in the North was possibly enforced by discouraging or restricting access to nonwhite users either through verbal means (perhaps comfort station attendants were instructed to prevent the entry of nonwhite users) or through placing comfort stations in locations that might be easily accessible only to white users. Either way, I have not so far found evidence of physically manifested segregation akin to what can be found in examples of southern comfort stations. Here, creators designed racial exclusion into the space. These differing sections of the comfort stations were certainly separate and unequal, offering more room and higher-quality accommodations for white users. Thus, these southern examples not only excluded by gender and race but also classed these categories through their physical design.

The racially segregated designs of the southern comfort stations, at least in one case, altered gendered divisions as well. In the facility in Paris, Texas, the "ladies" rest room and toilets were located on the main floor of the building, while the "gent's" toilet and rooms for "negro men" and "negro women" were all placed on the ground floor (see Figure 4.14). We can clearly infer that "ladies" and "gents" referred to white women and white men. The privacy of white women was quite literally placed above that of everyone else, reflecting middle-class society's ultimate concern with *white* women's bodies. Gender- and race-based exclusions reinforced each other in this comfort station and likely others.

Public Relief: Intended Use

By examining the design plans, layouts, and fixtures of these public comfort stations, we can gain a sense of how architects, planners, builders, and public officials intended to impress their understanding of privacy onto these physical spaces. But how were these spaces actually experienced by users? To begin to answer this question, it is essential to examine how comfort stations were actually used and, at times, misused by patrons. It is clear that these sites were, in fact, used and quite popular in several different cities. In 1905, a station in Cleveland served an average of four thousand patrons a day, while a station in Brooklyn served seven thousand patrons a day.[53] Six thousand patrons a day visited a Washington, DC, comfort station, while stations in Baltimore and Seattle averaged one thousand users a day. More than twelve million patrons found relief in one of Brooklyn's six comfort stations annually.[54]

An expected level of cleanliness and hygiene was also part of how privacy was understood by the middle-class creators of these spaces. Comfort station promoters connected these sanitary and hygienic goals with overall public health. As Chicago's health commissioner noted in 1915, "poor toilet facilities spread disease."⁵⁵ One periodical writer asked, "If as medical authorities claim, many dangerous and contagious diseases common today are directly traceable to [unsanitary conveniences], is it not a community sin for any city or town to neglect to provide public comfort stations fitted up with the latest approved sanitary appliances?"⁵⁶ By the early 1930s, the Women's City Club of New York offered photographic evidence of some of the city's dirty, neglected, and unsanitary public comfort stations. The club members pointed out that the use of outdated trough-style urinals and dark wooden toilet seats contributed to the filthy and unhygienic appearance of the comfort stations.

Middle-class reformers argued that these public toilet facilities should be "absolutely sanitary . . . [and] should present at all times a 'spotlessly white' appearance."⁵⁷ Municipal officials proposed plans for public toilet facilities to be created using light-colored materials, such as white glazed tiles and white enameled brick, "to avoid dust and to give the utmost light and cleanliness."⁵⁸ Comfort station proponents called for "toilet paper, liquid or powdered soap and paper towels to be available free at all times."⁵⁹ The availability of these items was understood as having a positive effect on patrons' personal hygiene. To maintain these stations, public officials called for educating users about the proper way to keep the facilities sanitary.⁶⁰

One plumbing supplies company advocated placing "foot stances" at the base of urinals, "indicating to users the proper place to stand." This "proper" foot placement likely prevented splashes, thus keeping the comfort station cleaner and more sanitary. These foot guides also prevented users from scratching the porcelain.⁶¹ The same company offered trough-style urinals with extra high backs in order "to prevent careless or mischievous persons from soiling the wall" of the comfort station. The designers and creators of these private spaces sought to materially impose their hygienic ideals on public comfort stations.

Early public restroom designers also fostered a moral understanding of privacy in creating these new spaces. Social commentators hoped these sites would not only improve cleanliness and hygiene but also be morally uplifting for the users. As one reformer argued, public toilet facilities needed to be designed and maintained in order to "create an atmosphere of absolute cleanliness and due regard for decorum."⁶² Social commentators connected the physical equipment and layout of these spaces to the morality of the patrons of the space. "Pure white glazed earthen fixtures set in pure white compartments foster[ed] a feeling of decency and aid[ed] in inducing cleanly habits," according to one engineer. And the very construction and maintenance of such sites could prove morally uplifting to those without other options. In fact, so many men patronized saloons to find relief that saloon owners noted that their toilet facilities generated more business than the free lunch.[63] Public toilet facilities offered a "moral" alternative by "the discouraging of the glass, taken often when not greatly desired, to recompense the saloon keeper."[64] Other commentators hoped city workers and street cleaners would avail themselves of these sites, as they were largely "foreign-born" and "lacked that fine sense which prevents their committing nuisances in alleys."[65] This middle-class understanding of morality became materialized within these spaces.

Public Relief: Misuse and Transgression

In the physical construction of early public restrooms, we can see how the creators of these sites understood privacy. But the actual experience of users of these sites may not have aligned with this understanding. The alternative use and even misuse of these spaces offers an opportunity to explore users' actual experiences. Since comfort stations afforded privacy in public, they also afforded the possibility for transgression. Commentators noted a number of ways these spaces were "misused" at the time. In fact, some of the later designs for public comfort stations sought to prevent unacceptable behavior through a physical redesign of the space. One of the preliminary problems noted by commentators was theft and defacement of the comfort station furnishings. As early as 1867, New York City instituted a $50 fine or three months in jail for "defacing or defiling" any public comfort station.[66] And in 1919, a Wisconsin law stated that "display of indecent pictures and writing in the stations will be punishable offenses."[67] By 1916, social commentators recommended that comfort stations "should have no loose or detachable parts liable to be tampered with or to be taken away" because, as one reformer noted, "vandals soil and destroy fixtures and fittings, while petty thieves pilfer removable parts and even wrench away fixed parts which they can sell."[68] One public official recommended designing the toilet seats so that no one would be able to stand on them, likely so that no one could hide in the stalls or peer over the walls at other patrons.[69] New York City officials banned "loud, profane or indecent language [and] boisterous or intoxicated persons" from the city's public comfort stations.[70] Under accusations of noncustomers "lounging," the "carelessness and lack of consideration shown by patrons," and overall "misuse" of their public toilet facilities (especially by women), department store managers began to scale down their elaborate restrooms.[71] One comfort station in New York appears to have installed toilet booths without doors, possibly in order to combat "petty larceny, careless use of fixtures and lounging by the unemployed and homeless"[72] (Figure 4.15). It is unclear whether these doorless stalls were located on the men's or women's side of the comfort station, but their installation does speak to the limits or "misuse" of privacy in public spaces.

Public comfort stations also became potential meeting places for illicit sexual activity, as documented by historian George Chauncey.[73] These activities were usually recorded only if the individuals were caught by law enforcement. For example, a police officer reported that "Frank Clark and Edward Mills committed a crime against nature" in the comfort station at City Hall Park in 1896.[74] They were found guilty of "sodomy," and their activities deemed in direct opposition to the "peace of the People of the State of New York, and their dignity."[75] Arthur Johnson and Louis Weismuller both maintained their innocence but were ultimately found guilty of "sodomy" in the same Central Park comfort station, also in 1896.[76] While these

Figure 4.15. Interior photo from Women's City Club of New York, *Comfort Stations of New York City: Today and Tomorrow* (New York: Women's City Club of New York, 1932). Reproduced with permission of the Women's City Club of New York.

individuals were "caught," it is reasonable to assume that many more weren't. And it is also likely that women, as well as men, found the privacy afforded by public comfort stations allowed them to perform private sexual activities in a discreet public place.

Social commentators were also concerned about crimes against comfort station users, and their discussions offer further insight into how these sites were actually experienced. One public official warned against locating comfort stations in isolated areas "for no better lurking place could be found for a foe."[77] It was suggested that station entrances be highly visible, with "the constant passing of pedestrians," to make them "self-policing, thus removing apprehension of danger in the use of these stations."[78] Architects began to design these spaces to prevent illicit activity, but this very privacy allowed for activities to take place that were usually prohibited in public spaces. The variety of activities that were performed in these spaces demonstrates the limits of privacy in these public places. These transgressions highlight the contradiction between the creators' definition of privacy and the public's actual experience of privacy through the use of the space.

Relief under Surveillance

The creators of public restrooms placed human regulators in these sites to reinforce the intended understanding of privacy. To bridge the gap between intention and reality, designers provided for a human element to this built environment in the form of comfort station attendants (Figure 4.16). In addition to the "thorough daily cleaning" necessitated by the "carelessness of its many users," public comfort station attendants also regulated and served as gatekeepers within these spaces.[79] Commentators acknowledged possible misuse by the station's patrons, making daily cleanings by attendants "necessary by the carelessness of the many users." Attendants were also to "be on constant lookout so that no loose or easily detached fittings [would be] appropriated and that no loitering or defacing of the walls [would take] place."[80] One commentator suggested giving attendants police powers.[81] Many public toilet facilities were designed with specific rooms for attendants to operate out of while on duty, thus providing constant surveillance.[82] In several New York public comfort stations, two or three attendants were on duty at the same time to regulate and clean high-traffic stations.[83] One commentator noted that male attendants, especially those on night duty, were "liable to encounter trouble from boisterous and abusive persons in an intoxicated con-

ONE OF NEW YORK'S COMFORT STATIONS
An admirable example of equipment and maintenance

Figure 4.16. "One of New York's Comfort Stations," from Donald B. Armstrong, "Public Comfort Stations: Their Economy and Sanitation," *American City* 11, no. 2 (August 1914): 95. Courtesy of the University of Delaware Library.

dition."[84] Attendants were also called on to remove homeless people who "occasionally enter free closets for the express purpose of spending the night in them."[85] Comfort station attendants were also given the authority to refuse entry to patrons the attendant deemed "unsanitary."[86] Often uniformed in white suits to match the light-colored fixtures of the stations, attendants functioned as human extensions of the architectural intentions of these spaces. While attendants paid "constant attention to the cleanliness of the station," "neatness" in their personal appearance was also required.[87] Attendants were another material component designers used to reinforce their specific definition of privacy. And the price of this intended privacy was a constant surveillance that limited users' experience of privacy.

Public comfort stations arose at the turn of the twentieth century to fulfill societal needs. Although they were novel spaces, they were designed, created, and regulated according to a middle-class understanding of privacy. Designers drew on distinctions of gender, class, and race as fundamental elements in shaping a sense of privacy within these public spaces. Middle-class beliefs about hygiene and morality were also built into these sites. But in noting the misuse of these spaces, we can gain a sense of the actual historical experience, not just the intended use, of these sites.

CHAPTER FIVE

Learning Privacy
Public School Locker Rooms

In 1912, a journalist who visited Painesdale High School described it as "undoubtedly the finest mining camp school in the United States" (Figure 5.1). This public high school, located in northern Michigan's copper mining region, was populated almost entirely by "children of wage earners [who would] probably become wage earners themselves." According to the journalist, "physical training is part of the course of every grade. It comes in for its allotted daily period just as regularly as does algebra or physics." The journalist witnessed female students taking part in "regular Swedish exercises for the strengthening of their bodies and the result is the Painesdale high school girls are a future generation of strong and graceful women." The journalist noted that the physical education regime "is carried up to the point of personal cleanliness of all pupils" as "every Monday, under proper supervision, every pupil ... takes a shower bath." According to the journalist, "an active mind in a healthy body ... might well be adopted as the motto of the school."[1]

These sentiments highlight the growing importance of public schooling and physical education at the turn of the twentieth century. In an increasingly industrial, urban, and populous United States, social commentators focused their attention on improving the lives of the nation's youth. Middle-class reformers argued that public school physical education and hygiene programs could counter the adverse effects of urban and industrial life on the children of working-class, immigrant families. These reformers connected the mental and moral development of America's youth with their physical health and hygiene. The development of the public school system and the growing importance of physical education and hygiene necessitated the creation of new private spaces where students could cleanse and clothe their bodies at school.[2]

Figure 5.1. "High School, Painesdale, Mich.," n.d., MS-019-04-05-02, Brockway Photograph Collection, Michigan Technological University Archives and Copper Country Historical Collections.

Public school locker rooms were one of the first private spaces created specifically for children. Here we can examine how designers incorporated their definition of privacy into a space where the primary users were minors. Societies tend to find it more acceptable to control the behavior and experiences of children than to do the same with adults. This spatial case study demonstrates how far design could go to control the private acts of users in public places.

Public school locker rooms were spaces of socialization. This chapter builds on the earlier discussion of public baths by analyzing attempts to use the design of public school locker rooms to inculcate children into the designers' middle-class understanding of privacy. But in this case, the power differential between users and creators was even more pronounced. Contemporary social norms deemed that children held an inferior status to adults. Public school locker rooms were created and used to teach adolescents how to function within similar private spaces in public places. Within school locker rooms and baths, young men and women learned how to perform the private activities of dressing, undressing, and cleansing and relieving their bodies in the presence of nonfamilial adults and peers.

Public school locker rooms were also spaces of surveillance, ensuring that students adhered to the middle-class social norms they were being taught.

Students' inferior position, due to their age and subordinate status, permitted school officials, teachers, coaches, and attendants to coerce students into performing private activities, including changing clothing and bathing, within the public space of the locker room. Many public school students were from working-class and immigrant families, reinforcing their subordinate status. This chapter will explore how differing male and female experiences of the locker room formed the foundation for educating public school students about the middle-class understanding of privacy. To fully appreciate the varying experiences of these early locker rooms, this chapter will incorporate first-person accounts from former students who attended Painesdale High School in the 1930s.

The Growth of Public Education

The emergence of public schools, and their attendant physical education programs, created a need for spaces that would permit private acts, such as bathing, dressing, undressing, and relieving oneself, in what was otherwise a public setting. The creation of public school locker rooms was directly related to the increase in public schooling in the late nineteenth and early twentieth centuries. In 1850, there were only eleven public schools in the nation. But by the end of the Civil War, most states had established a public school system, and nearly 50 percent of American children were enrolled.[3] As the nineteenth century wore on, social commentators, public officials, and reformers became eager to instill "republican," "American" principles and middle-class values in the growing masses of the urban industrial working class through their children.[4] As one contemporary social commentator noted, "unless children come into contact with American life through the public school, they're likely to grow up ignorant of American institutions and thoroughly unfit for citizenship."[5] Reformers called for "the end of the doctrine of laissez-faire with reference to the Americanization of the immigrant."[6] And US public education expanded to meet the needs of the growing population and the goals of Progressive reformers during the early twentieth century. Overall public school enrollment grew from 15.5 million in 1900 to 25.7 million in 1950.[7] Enrollment in public high schools alone rose from 519,000 students in 1900 to 5.7 million in 1950. Public schools also became the largest budget expenditure for many communities.[8] This growth in public school populations was also the result of stronger compulsory education laws passed from the 1890s through the 1920s. Although there were compulsory education laws "on the books" before this time, the later laws were actually enforceable and therefore more effective.[9]

Prior to the Civil War, most public education took place in single-room schoolhouses, where students of various ages and education levels were taught by a single teacher. In the second half of the nineteenth century, school reformers began to argue that "age-grading" would allow students to learn at a pace appropriate for their psychological development.[10] By the turn of the twentieth century, psychologists argued that adolescence was a distinct developmental stage between childhood and adulthood, resulting in the need to further separate younger children from older ones.[11] At the same time, school reformers spoke in favor of consolidating school resources in larger school districts to pool tax revenue and students in larger, age-graded school buildings.[12]

Larger, modern school buildings were created to accommodate the growing public school population in the early twentieth century. Painesdale High School offers an example of an early modern public school. It opened in 1909 and accommodated four hundred students.[13] The school housed an assembly hall, recitation rooms, science labs, a manual training room where boys learned carpentry, and a domestic science room where girls were taught cooking and sewing skills.[14] Significantly, students were provided with a gymnasium and boys' and girls' locker rooms with showers. The school was later renovated in 1933 to expand the physical educational area to include a swimming pool and larger gymnasium.[15] The school's principal, Cora Jeffers, taught herself to swim in order to instruct the female students in this essential component of physical education at the school.[16]

Physical Education in Public Schools

Contemporary reformers perceived public schools as a means of educating working-class and immigrant students in middle-class "American" values. But these reformers also recognized the opportunity to physically socialize students through physical education programs and their associated spaces. As public education grew, educators, social commentators, and reformers argued that it was necessary to train the students physically as well as mentally. Educators and reformers grew concerned about students' physical development because of the amount of time students were spending inactively seated at their desks in these newly emerging public schools, a consequence of an increasingly urban and industrial United States.[17] After the onset of World War I, physical education proponents argued for the need "to promote the physical fitness of our youth if we are to be a nation strong for peace-time production and strong again in the emergency of war," thereby tying the bodily health of American youth to the health of the nation as a whole.[18] In 1921, the head of the National Physical Education Service stated that "physical education [is] a tremendous force working directly for the promotion of happiness and power for service and also working indirectly ... by increasing productive power, ... and laying the basis for a powerful and independent nation."[19] One critic of the era went even further, claiming that physical education and personal hygiene needed to be a part of the public school curriculum "to reinforce the physical stamina of the race."[20] Dean Cole, a former student at Painesdale High School, recalled the school's yearly community exhibition of students' physical fitness, with students performing feats of strength with dumbbells as well as choreographed dance routines.[21] Such school displays of physical education programs served to highlight the importance of students' physical training to the public.

Reformers and educators also based their arguments for including physical education in the public school curriculum on the need for "well-rounded" student bodies and the developing belief in a mind-body connection.[22] As one physician noted, "bathing, like other measures ... of physical hygiene may be an important phase of mental hygiene [as] the psychical effect of a sense of physical cleanliness is evident to all."[23] Another argued, "exercise has for its aims the promotion of health and the acquisition of correct habits of action."[24] In one study of students who were required to bathe at school every morning, the instructor noted that the children had "lost the air of languor that characterized them at first and are [now] fond of work and abreast of their grades."[25] Contemporary commentators directly related the intellectual education of students to their physical education and justified the need for new programs and spaces where students would learn about the proper care and maintenance of their bodies.

Physical education proponents couched their arguments for new sites for physical education within the modern middle class's social concerns. Proponents hoped that by training students' bodies as well as their minds, public schools would be able to mitigate the perceived adverse effects of the industrializing and urbanizing American environment.[26] One educator, in 1912, voiced concern that "modern city life ha[d] produced conditions which tend to destroy the physical fitness of the coming generation."[27] Another educator argued that children living in urban environments were "often nervous and self-conscious" because of noise, lack of sleep, eating too many sweets, lack of fresh air, and "mee[ting] too many people and hav[ing] no chance to be alone and rest."[28] By the early twentieth century, these ideas were becoming formalized. In 1925, the National Education Association called for a gymnasium in all junior and senior high schools, and by 1930, thirty-nine states had passed physical education laws.[29]

In addition to gymnasiums where students learned to train their bodies, social commentators also argued for the creation of attendant-monitored locker rooms and bathing spaces where students would learn to properly clean and dress their bodies. Physical education programs created an opportunity to expose a lack of personal hygiene in the poor and working classes (an issue that preoccupied social reformers at the time). These middle-class commentators questioned the hygiene of the working-class body and often the immigrant body more specifically. Reformers contrasted the overall cleanliness of working-class immigrants' homes, clothing, and bodies with those of "native-born," middle-class Americans.[30] Contemporary critics argued that cleansing immigrants' bodies would improve their overall hygiene, thus making them more "American."[31] According to one social commentator, daily bathing "had a very beneficial effect on the foreign element."[32] He noted that, in Boston, immigrant women who bathed regularly "[did] not neglect their children so much, and the boys and girls seen playing do not have the dirty faces, the unkempt hair, and the tattered and soiled clothing formerly a common sight in the Boston slums."[33] Reformers hoped that physically training public school students and requiring them to cleanse their bodies at school would lead students to carry these hygienic habits home with them. This agenda was reinforced by inspecting how well children carried out their "homework." In 1916, New York City elementary school teachers were encouraged to "[conduct] daily morning health inspections and toothbrush drills" and promote "home hygiene" in the largely working-class, immigrant populations of their schools.[34] In addition to teaching the children of immigrants to read and write, reformers hoped to "Americanize" immigrants' bodies through physical education.

The spaces for physical education were created for students who were considered subordinate not just because of their age but often also because of their class and ethnicity. There was often a class-based and ethnic experience of private activities within these public school locker rooms. Commentators noted that in areas where the majority of the population was "foreign born," public school students carried the cleanliness they learned in the locker rooms back home to their families.³⁵ In 1904, the Free Bath Commission of Baltimore found that "one of the gravest problems in school sanitation in the larger cities, and especially in schools situated in the poorer sections . . . [is] secur[ing] cleanliness in the dress and person of children coming from houses which are but poorly provided with facilities for bathing."³⁶ According to one reformer, the Paul Revere School and its bathing facilities were ideally located in a densely populated area of Boston "consisting mainly of Hebrews and Italians, with a liberal percentage of other nationalities."³⁷ Prior to the creation of dedicated bathing facilities within schools, some urban schools "conducted parties of school children" to the closest public bath.³⁸ By cleansing and regulating the bodies of children of working-class immigrants, educators and school officials hoped to "Americanize" students' families by extension.

For their part, working-class parents did not appear to have been opposed to these new programs. Dean Cole, his brother Walter Cole, and their classmate Elnore Saaranen never recalled any parents complaining about their school's bathing regime or physical education program.³⁹ Like many industrial workers at the time, their fathers utilized the free bathing facilities offered to them at the mining company's dryhouses or change houses (Figure 5.2). Here, the miners were offered washbasins, showers, and baths, as well as lockers similar to those found in the high school locker room. Because their husbands always came home clean from the mine, miners' wives appreciated the change house as well.⁴⁰ In the case of Painesdale, the dryhouse and high school were built around the same time, making such bathing facilities a part of everyday life for miners and their families.⁴¹

But the initial implementation of locker rooms and bathing facilities was not without opposition. Those opposed to these new spaces questioned the propriety of offering spaces for students to conduct the private activities of bathing, dressing, and undressing within a public school. The Boston School Board initially objected to adding showers to the design of the Paul Revere School in 1898. Members were concerned that it was not the "duty of the school authorities to bathe children . . . because they may not be clean."⁴² They argued that if schools started taking responsibility for bathing children, this obligation would be extended to clothing students or even "feeding [students] if not properly nourished at home."⁴³ Other critics expressed concerns about the costs of bathing students, children catching cold after bathing, and whether "school was not the place to educate children to appreciate the

Figure 5.2. "Allouez #2 Shaft Change House," 1915–1916. Calumet & Hecla Photograph Collection, Michigan Technological University Archives and Copper Country Historical Collections.

cleanliness obtained by bathing."[44] But supporters of bathing facilities in public schools noted improvements in student learning that resulted from regular school baths.[45]

The ultimate argument for creating locker rooms and bathing facilities in public schools was that most public school children in the early twentieth century did not have access to private bathing facilities in their homes.[46] Thus, providing immigrant, working-class children with "proper" bathing facilities in public school locker rooms and coercing them to use these facilities became central to Progressives' push to expand the public school system. These middle-class reformers saw physical education and school bathing facilities as a way to influence public school students and their families, who were often members of the working class.[47] As one commentator noted, school bathing facilities were unnecessary in schools "located in good neighborhoods and attended by the children of people who [were] tolerably well-to-do and in whose homes cleanliness [was] usually attained."[48] Children "of the poorer classes" were accused of degrading the overall cleanliness of school buildings because of their "utter disregard for, and lack of personal cleanliness" due to the dearth of proper bathing facilities in their homes.[49] Some schools kept lists of students whose homes had no bathing facilities "or whose parents [were] too ignorant or too indifferent to give them proper care."[50] School administrators noted success in their endeavors as some "parents awakened to the fact that the children must be clean, and if they do not make them so someone else will."[51] Reformer and photographer Lewis Hine captured one such child bathing in a laundry tub in a the common kitchen of a tenement building in 1908 (Figure 5.3).

Physical education spaces were created and designed with the assumption that students would need to be taught how to properly care for and clean their bodies. In addition to keeping classrooms more sanitary and helping students learn to "appreciate cleanliness," social reformers hoped that the experience of dressing and undressing in school locker rooms would have "the effect of making [students] more tidy in regards to their undergarments."[52] The peer pressure of the locker room would have "a beneficial influence in the children's homes for parents [would] naturally strive to keep their children cleaner and their garments neater when they know that in undressing together slovenliness of dress or raggedness of underclothes, due to the mother's carelessness or inattention, may reflect unfavorably on the children."[53] One school bath attendant "criticized, in a kindly way, the torn or unclean underwear" of some students and "suggested that the owners bring clean garments for bathing day."[54] She also "removed all the superfluous hair from the heads of the boys" and "comb[ed] the girls' hair, teaching them to keep it neat."[55] As with personal cleanliness in the larger society at the time, students' hygiene was linked to their moral character. Social commentators asked, "Is it not a fact that . . . lack of cleanliness leads to loss of

Figure 5.3. Lewis Hine, "Bath in Laundry Tub in Tenement Kitchen," 1908. Courtesy of Museum of Fine Arts, Boston, Gift of Naomi and Walter Rosenblum, 1980: 297. Photograph © 2021 Museum of Fine Arts, Boston.

self-respect, to bad habits, vulgarity and vice?"[56] Others called for instruction on temperance to be a part of personal hygiene courses.[57]

Dean Cole offered a firsthand example of several teachers who took their lesson about personal hygiene a bit too far. According to Dean, "a lot of the [local] families were fairly poor at that time." Upon entering high school, a young boy from a working-class Finnish family was singled out by three male teachers who "noticed that this boy's underwear was so bad that they decided to take it upon themselves to keep him after school one night." Dean recalled that the teachers bought the boy new "winter underwear" with their own money at the mining company's store. Then, according to Dean, "they took his old underwear and they took him in the shower and gave him a shower. But the next day, [the boy's] father came to the school and he threw the underwear back at the teachers." Dean said that boy's father "was so proud, it was an embarrassment to him." Dean remembered, "it was all over town and those teachers got reprimanded by Mrs. Jeffers [the high school principal]." (Dean also recalled, as an aside, that this boy's sister sat in front of him in one of his classes and he could "see lice jumping off her braids.")[58]

Educators and reformers believed that inspections of the students' bodies were necessary to treat and prevent the spread of disease, illness, and unhygienic practices.[59] Therefore, the newly created physical education spaces would need to allow for the surveillance of students and their physical habits. One commentator noted in a contemporary medical journal that "shower baths for public schools are needed.... The required use of them would have a very beneficent influence on the prevailing spread of contagion[s]."[60] In the public school locker room, children were taught how to bathe, care for their bodies, and even dress and maintain their clothing.[61] For Elnore, Dean, and Walter, children of working-class parents, this meant learning to cleanse themselves daily with soap and towels provided by their school.[62] School bathing attendants often "exercised keen observation for any symptoms of skin disease [and] held children responsible for progress made in any direction."[63] The public schools administration prescribed "regular washing and combing to eradicate vermin," and students' "mothers were sent for and instructed to clean the beds."[64] Many of them were ready and able to cooperate with the school authorities.[65] It was assumed that these students came from homes and families that did not provide them with the necessary means for properly and hygienically maintaining their bodies.

Locker rooms were designed to achieve gender segregation but also to adhere to different gendered expectations about private acts. Not only were boys and girls separated physically, but the girls' spaces were designed in a way that made it possible for them to achieve physical separation from one another, whereas boys' spaces were designed with communal showers that made it possible for an external observer to monitor their behavior in the private act of dressing or bathing. Designers also located instructor offices in these spaces, enabling direct observation of bathing, dressing, and undressing by external observers who monitored the minor students' behavior, as well as their bodies. This experience of being watched prepared adolescents for similar surveillance in the private spaces in public places they would experience in the future as adults.

Learning Privacy: Physical Education Spaces

Public school locker rooms were built to expose children to middle-class understandings of physical fitness, hygiene, and, most important, privacy. In these spaces, public school students learned that privacy was based on a physical separation of female and male bodies. Emerging sites of physical education exposed middle-class concerns about physical hygiene, fitness, and the effects of industrialization, immigration, and urbanization. Locker rooms and bathing facilities were developed to inculcate middle-class values about bodily privacy into the largely working-class, ethnically diverse student population of the emerging public school system. The differing experiences of boys and girls formed the foundation of this lesson about privacy.

Gendered Spaces

As with public restrooms, department store dressing rooms, and public baths, newly emerging spaces for physical education were designed to create a private space in a public place. Just as with the spaces discussed in previous chapters, gender segregation was foundational in creating the middle-class understanding of privacy in these emerging spaces. School buildings in the early twentieth century were designed to separate the private space of the locker room along gender lines. These buildings further separated students by gender in the physical spaces of the gymnasium and pool.[66] Often, girls' and boys' locker rooms were placed on opposite sides of the school building, with totally separate entrances.[67] Some schools offered entirely different gymnasiums, outdoor playgrounds, and pools for boys and girls (Figures 5.4 and 5.5).[68] Other schools were designed with separate playrooms, hallways, and coatrooms for boys and girls, reinforcing the notion that physical play and putting on or taking off one's outerwear were bodily activities that needed to be gender segregated.[69] And in some instances, all students used the same gymnasiums and swimming pools, but boys and girls used these facilities at different times in gender-segregated gym and swimming classes (Figure 5.6).[70] This gender segregation in public schools appeared to be taken for granted by 1909, as one school architect noted that "toilets . . . for the two sexes should, of course, be as completely and widely separated as possible."[71]

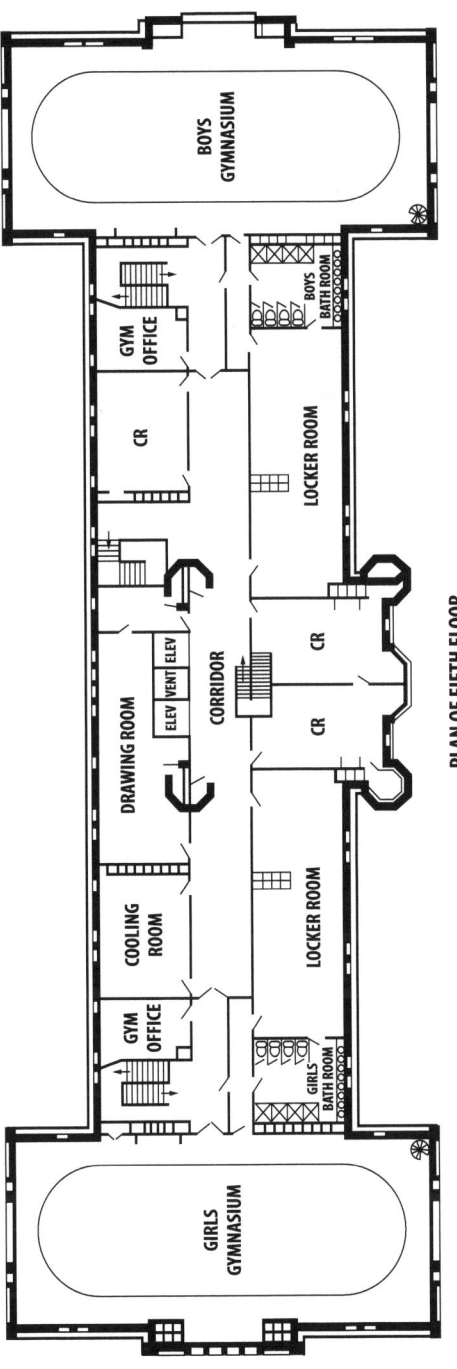

PLAN OF FIFTH FLOOR

Figure 5.4. Based on C. B. J. Snyder, architectural plan for the Peter Cooper High School, New York City, in G. W. Wharton, "High School Architecture in the City of New York," *School Review* 11, no. 6 (June 1903): 476. Redrawn by Jade Myers.

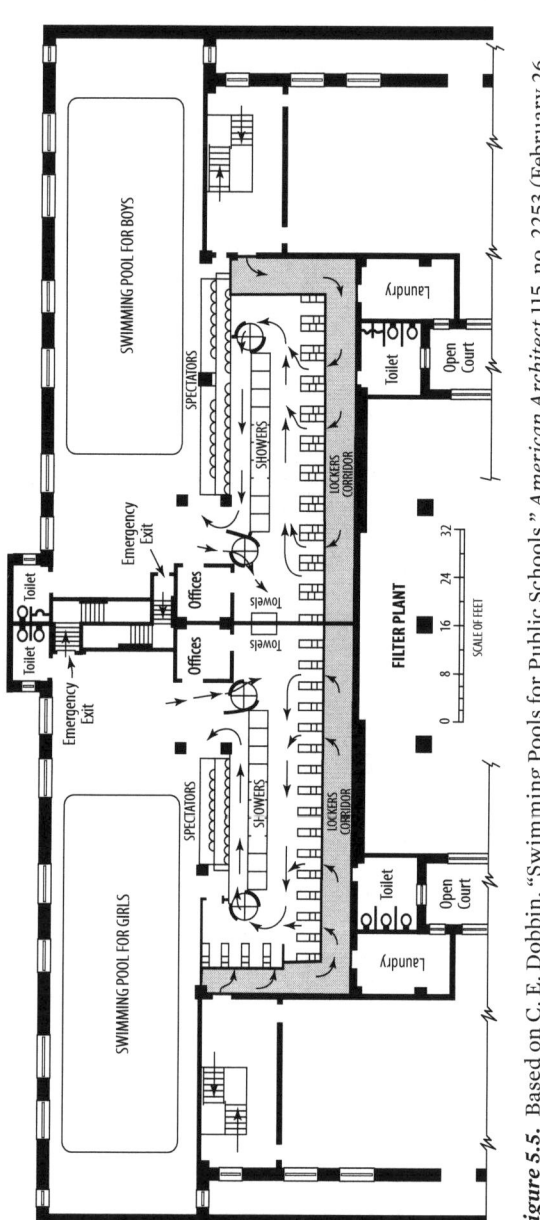

Figure 5.5. Based on C. E. Dobbin, "Swimming Pools for Public Schools," *American Architect* 115, no. 2253 (February 26, 1919): 322. Redrawn by Jade Myers.

Figure 5.6. "A Tennis Court and Playground on the Roof of a Public School in the Borough of Manhattan," from J. Harold Braddock, "Using City Roofs for Public Health and Recreation," *American City* 10, no. 2 (February 1914): 138. Courtesy of the University of Delaware Library.

American adolescents were thus taught that gender was an essential component of bodily privacy.

The boys' and girls' locker rooms at Painesdale High School were located at opposite ends of the gym and connected to the swimming pool via separate entrances. Dean noted that, after a required shower, with soap provided by the school, students passed through recessed terrazzo footbaths to "sanitize your feet and make sure you weren't carrying any germs." Although boys and girls used the same swimming pool, they had gender-segregated swim classes (Figure 5.7).[72]

But separate classes was only the beginning of these differing gendered experiences. As we have seen in other private spaces in public places, very different spaces were created for female and male bodies. In these physical education spaces, girls and boys learned that not only were their bodies different, but middle-class society placed very different expectations on them. Girls were issued a school swimsuit and swimming cap. "I hated [the cap] because I would set my hair in a pageboy style, and swimming was during second hour," Elnore Saaranen recalled. "And of course they made you go

Figure 5.7. Natatorium, Painesdale High School, Painesdale, Michigan (built in 1933), photograph by Jeremiah Mason, July 2010.

right under the water, but we tried not to so our hair wouldn't get wet. But we would end up with scraggly hair the rest of the day."[73] The boys, however, were not issued swimming suits and caps. "At that time, the boys always swam nude," remembered Dean. (But Walter noted that the girls' suits were "nothing more than what you'd see in a wet T-shirt contest.") At the end of the boys' morning swim classes, the school's female principal would walk partway down the girls' entrance to the pool and blow a whistle to signal that it was time for the boys to return to the locker rooms so that the girls' swim class could begin. But this gendered pool exchange didn't always go according to plan. Walter recalled that "on a number of occasions . . . she didn't give [the boys] enough time, and the girls would come running in there." To cover themselves, the boys would swim up against the side of the pool.[74]

Gender difference was further reinforced because the physical space of public school locker-room facilities often varied drastically according to gender. Some girls' locker rooms were equipped with individual stall showers, whereas their male counterparts were subjected to communal shower rooms.[75] One school architect argued that "for girls, bathing suits and separate bathing and dressing compartments are necessary." Older girls especially required "greater privacy in dressing and undressing."[76] But this level of privacy for boys was "not only unnecessary but undesirable."[77] At a Boston public school, the girls' bathing facilities contained individual dressing rooms with seats and "self-closing blind door[s]" in addition to individual shower stalls.[78] Boys, on the other hand, showered twelve at a time in a group shower and dressed in a common dressing room (Figure 5.8).[79]

Hair dryers were sometimes installed in girls' locker rooms but not on the boys' side. In some locker rooms, girls were afforded more benches and lockers than boys were. In addition, restrooms attached to the locker rooms offered girls individual toilet stalls, while the boys' restrooms afforded one stall with several urinals. To accommodate these features, some girls' locker rooms were larger than boys. Girls were, at times, given more physical space and more private space in their locker rooms than boys.[80] Girls were also given more time to undress, bathe, dry, and dress themselves than their male counterparts.[81] Thus, children were taught that not only gender segregation but also gender difference were essential to the dominant middle-class understanding of privacy. And the bodily privacy afforded each group differed, as did their experiences in their locker rooms. Girls were taught that their bodies required more seclusion and concealment (even from one another). Boys were taught that their bodies could be more visible, less hidden (as long as there were no females around).

Spaces for Surveillance

Just as physical education spaces were designed to separate and differentiate students according to gender, these sites were also designed to explicitly monitor students as they performed the private acts of dressing, undressing, and bathing. This surveillance was not only accepted but expected by the creators of these spaces, an expectation that differs from the adult spaces discussed earlier. Surveillance space usually took the form of an office for physical education instructors (Figure 5.9). The inclusion of teachers' offices within the locker rooms underscored the constant observance students experienced in these spaces. School architects called for the locker rooms to be laid out so that "those in charge may observe all that is going on from any position."[82]

Once locker-room facilities were installed in schools, instructors would make sure students were using them by monitoring their movements before, during, and after required physical education sessions. Students at the Painesdale High School bathed once a week and were "marched to this function as to

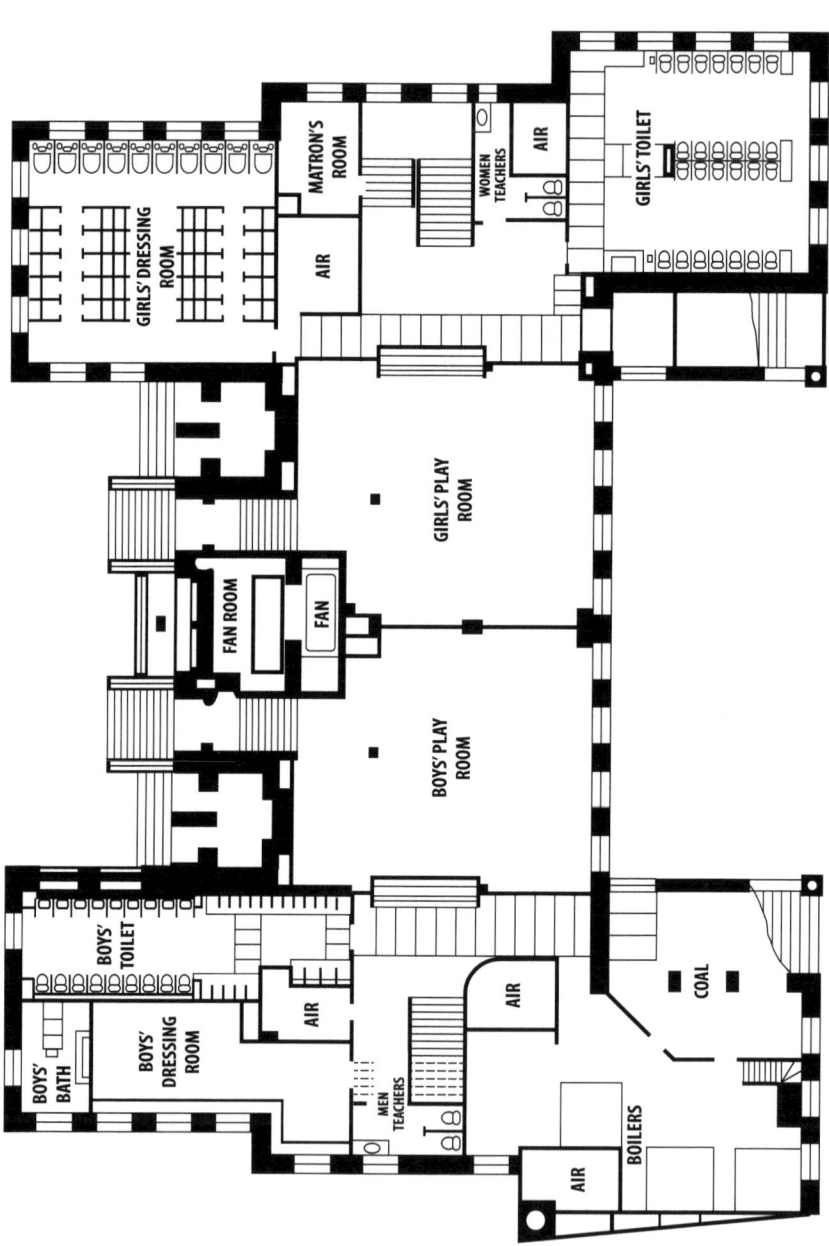

Figure 5.8. Based on "Plans, Paul Revere School, Boston, Mass.," from Edmund W. Wheelwright, "The American Schoolhouse, IV," *The Brickbuilder* 7, no. 4 (April 1898): 74. Redrawn by Jade Myers.

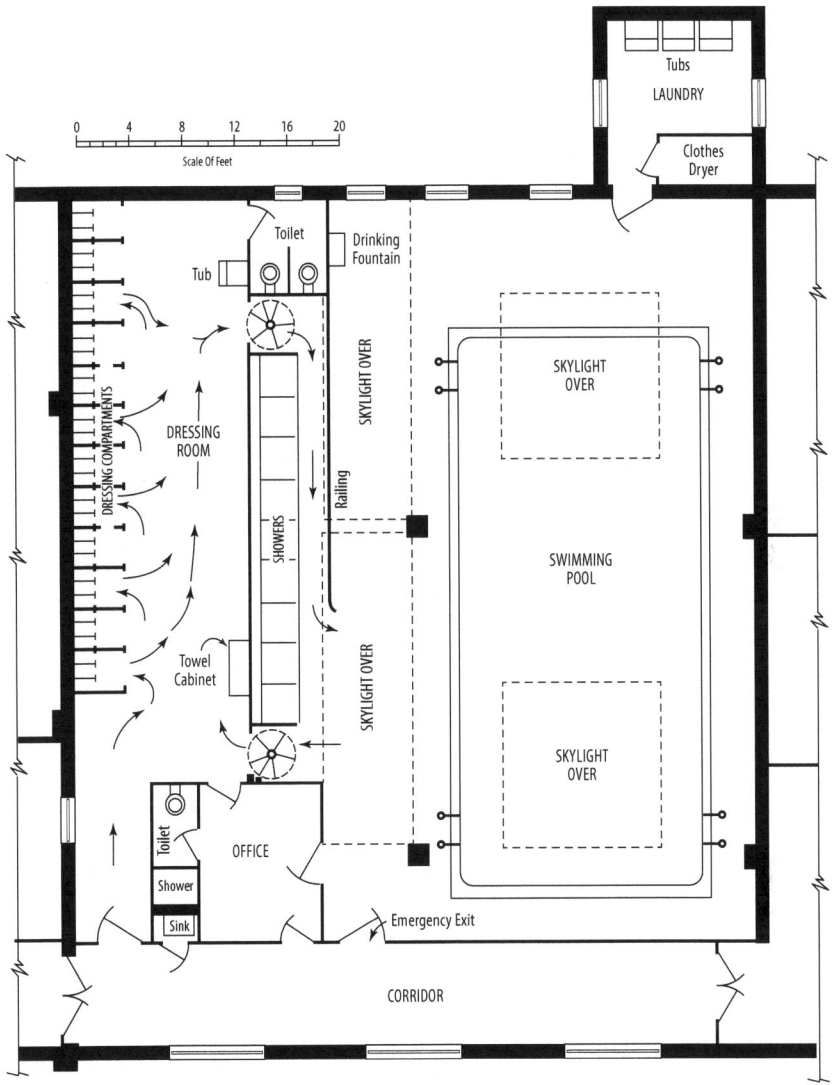

Figure 5.9. Based on "Natatorium in Public School No. 32, The Bronx," from C. E. Dobbin, "Swimming Pools for Public Schools," *American Architect* 115, no. 2253 (February 26, 1919): 320. Redrawn by Jade Myers.

every other recitation and only a grave reason, backed by a physician's certificate, [would] permit a student to forgo [their shower]."[83] Elnore noted that, although they had individual shower stalls, girls at Painesdale High School were required to shower and that there was "always a teacher there, somebody watching" (Figure 5.10).[84]

There was always a male instructor present in the boys' locker room at Painesdale as well, and according to Walter, their swimming instructor had an office inside the boys' locker room. It was, of course, much easier to keep

Figure 5.10. Girls' showers in locker room, Painesdale High School, Painesdale, Michigan (built in 1933), photograph by Jeremiah Mason, July 2010.

an eye on the boys because their locker room had a communal shower in which all of the boys showered together in one room (Figure 5.11).[85]

Dean recalled that this constant supervision limited any "horseplay," although Walter noted the occasional "snapping of towels." At another school, the girls' physical education instructor stood on a platform in the locker room so that she could "see the head and shoulders of each girl and make sure she [was] taking a shower before donning her suit."[86] Other schools conducted "inspection[s] of the physical condition" of students during bathing.[87] Some schools employed locker attendants to provide "constant supervision" within these spaces.[88] Female and male instructors were assigned to teach girls and boys separately for physical education classes, and they regulated corresponding locker rooms as well.[89] Elnore recalled that although students were given individual lockers to hang up their gym clothes, these lockers were never locked, allowing school officials constant access to these "private" spaces.[90] The physical design and layout of these spaces allowed teachers to monitor and regulate student behavior within these sites, with students' subordinate status due to their age used to justify such surveillance.

Figure 5.11. Boys' showers in locker room, Painesdale High School, Painesdale, Michigan (built in 1933), photograph by Jeremiah Mason, July 2010.

Learning Privacy: Cleansing the Student Body

The example of the public school locker room demonstrates that society's concepts of privacy can sometimes collide with other social expectations. One example is the need to monitor the behavior of children and the appropriateness of violating their privacy in order to do so. Other expectations about privacy, however, could clearly not be violated, such as gender segregation and higher modesty standards for women and girls. The value of these privacy aspects becomes clear when they are maintained in the design of these spaces, even as the need for authority figures to monitor behavior in these private areas persists. We gain insight into society's delineation of boundaries when these expectations come into conflict.

The issues surrounding the American working-class (often immigrant) body converged at the site of public school physical education facilities during the early twentieth century. Middle-class reformers saw locker rooms as sites of socialization for the children of the working class. In these spaces, students were taught the proper way to conduct the private activities of bathing and caring for their bodies. And at the center of the adolescent encounter with these newly created locker rooms was the experience of bodily privacy, as controlled by middle-class school administrators. In shaping, designing, and regulating these spaces, middle-class reformers and school officials controlled students' bodies by allowing varying levels of bodily privacy, especially according to gender. In this way, students learned the importance of gender segregation to the middle-class definition of privacy. But because of their subordinate status due to their age and class, students also learned how to perform private activities in a public space under middle-class-prescribed supervision and instruction.

The experiences of Elnore Saaranen and Dean and Walter Cole in the private space of the public school locker room offer personal examples of how adolescent bodies were regulated in the early twentieth century. Middle-class reformers and educators utilized the space of the locker room to instill their beliefs about gender, health, hygiene, and privacy in the largely working-class, often immigrant, students at America's growing public schools. Young men and women learned how to perform the private activities of dressing, undressing, cleansing, and relieving their bodies in the public space of the school locker room.

Students were taught the importance of gender segregation, regular physical exercise, and frequent soap-and-water showers in specialized bathing spaces. Students learned that the experience of privacy differed along gender, class, and ethnic lines and that, as adolescents, their privacy was a partial privacy, as teachers regularly monitored students' private activities. As public restrooms, dressing rooms, and baths were increasingly ubiquitous during this time, America's youth were introduced to these private/public spaces through their school locker rooms.

Conclusion

Privacy is a socially contested construct. At the turn of the twentieth century, this contest played out in a series of newly emerging spaces. Department store fitting rooms, public baths, public school locker rooms, and restrooms were created to offer privacy in public. These spaces could have been produced in a variety of ways, but the specific designs and layouts reveal the physical and social construction of these spaces. The designers and creators of these sites were usually from the middle class, and thus their definition of privacy became materially manifested. The middle-class understanding of privacy was based on physical and social exclusion, a definition that is exposed when we "read" these spaces. Middle-class society created fitting rooms, public baths, restrooms, and school locker rooms to prescribe that people should visually separate themselves from the rest of the public when performing the activities of dressing and undressing, bathing, and relieving their bodies. The middle-class designers and creators also socially constructed these spaces to exclude and segregate bodies according to gender, race, class, and age.

Department store fitting rooms began to appear at the end of the nineteenth century and are one of the first examples of a private space in a public place. Here, we can see how middle-class designers first grappled with creating privacy in public. Gender segregation formed the foundation for this privacy. By excluding men from women's clothing sections and fitting rooms, designers and executives hoped to align women's department store experiences with earlier, female-centric clothing traditions.

The public bathing movement exposed the stark contrasts in the way different social classes experienced privacy. Here, we can compare the new dedicated bathrooms in middle-class houses with the public baths provided for the working class. The middle class used the ultimate exclusion in their home bathing spaces to further distinguish themselves from the working class. Though public baths still offered gender (and, at times, age) exclusion, these baths were still inherently public. Members of the working class needed to leave their homes to bathe their bodies, while their middle-class counterparts could retreat to the inner sanctums of their own homes and bathe completely alone. The public bath was a space of condescension, where those in power (government officials, company executives, middle-class reformers, etc.) instructed users how best to bathe their working-class bodies.

The creation of the first public toilet facilities in the Unites States offers an opportunity to examine how middle-class designers created a public privacy based on gender, class, and racial exclusion. Analyzing early public restrooms allows us to delve into users' experiences as they engaged with these facilities. Often, these experiences were considered transgressive or as misuse because they deviated from the intentions of middle-class designers for these novel spaces. Municipal officials responded to instances of misuse by monitoring restrooms through hiring attendants or calling for police officers to patrol the sites. Sometimes users' transgressions resulted in redesigning the space itself. Early public restrooms uncover a spatial dialogue between users and creators.

Finally, in public school locker rooms, adolescents were "taught" a specifically middle-class meaning of privacy. In the early twentieth century, many public school students were members of the working class and were often the children of immigrants. These factors, combined with their age, resulted in an inferior status to their teachers and school administrators. As a result, public school locker rooms became a space of socialization through surveillance. Through instruction and constant supervision, students learned how to function in these newly created private spaces in public places.

Taken together, the spatial case studies presented here offer a glimpse into how middle-class reformers, designers, and creators instituted their definition of privacy at the turn of the twentieth century. Evidence of their beliefs about privacy is revealed not only in their self-conscious arguments for these spaces but also in the materiality of the spaces themselves. Gender, racial, and class exclusions formed the core tenets of this middle-class vision of privacy. But by creating private spaces for public use, these sites opened the door for transgression against this prescribed meaning of privacy.

Today the contest over privacy continues, and private spaces in public places continue to be at the center of this debate. Many of these spaces remain in use today. Our use of these spaces continues to be monitored and surveilled, revealing a continued societal apprehension about providing privacy in public.

We use these private spaces in public places to perform the same activities for which they were initially created: to relieve, cleanse, and clothe our bodies. The human body itself has, in many ways, remained constant, even as how society views those bodies, or even how we understand our bodies, has changed. Privacy remains highly valued today, even if how we define, understand, and experience it has changed. We are no less concerned with privacy than Victorian Americans were. We even have a new space to apply this concept to: the digital world. The debate over the meaning of privacy online is just as hotly contested as the debate over physical privacy.

In some very essential ways, these spaces have become outmoded. The assumption that these sites should be binarily gender segregated can be traced back to the initial emergence of these private spaces more than a century ago. The ubiquity of gender segregation across all of these historical examples underscores just how elemental gender division was to middle-class creators at that time. But our twenty-first century understanding of gender is far more complex and fluid. As society questions the binary nature of gender, we've also come to question the gender segregation these spaces were founded upon. In newly created or freshly redesigned examples of public toilets, single-user spaces attempt to sidestep the question of gender division by offering privacy to one user at a time. These individual-use spaces pose new questions: Could total exclusivity actually be more inclusive? Can complete privacy be achieved only when we are alone?

Recently, the COVID-19 pandemic highlighted just how porous these spatial boundaries are and just how illusory privacy in public can be, as invisible microbes added an additional concern to the use of these private spaces in public. By examining the birth of these spaces, we can begin to understand our current assumptions about these sites. The need for these facilities seems obvious, but the way in which they were created reveals much more. As we proceed through a new century and a new millennium, we have the opportunity to redesign these spaces and redefine our concept of privacy in the process.

NOTES

Chapter 1 • Privacy in Public

1. Public Facilities Privacy and Security Act, House Bill 2, General Assembly of North Carolina, March 23, 2016, http://www.ncleg.net/Sessions/2015E2/Bills/House/PDF/H2v1.pdf.

2. An Act Prohibiting Persons from Entering Single and Multiple Occupancy Restrooms or Changing Areas and Other Facilities in Elementary and Secondary Schools That Do Not Correspond with the Person's Biological Sex and Including Effective Date Provisions, Senate File 482, State of Iowa General Assembly, March 22, 2023, https://www.legis.iowa.gov/legislation/BillBook?ba=SF482&ga=90; Senate Bill 1100, Idaho Legislature, March 22, 2023, https://legislature.idaho.gov/sessioninfo/2023/legislation/s1100/; An Act to Amend the Criminal Offense of Sexual Indecency with a Child, Senate Bill 270, General Assembly of the State of Arkansas, March 29, 2023, https://www.arkleg.state.ar.us/Home/FTPDocument?path=%2FBills%2F2023R%2FPublic%2FSB270.pdf.

3. An Act Relating to Facility Requirements Based on Sex, Committee Substitute / House Bill 1521, Florida House of Representatives, 2023, https://www.flsenate.gov/Session/Bill/2023/1521/BillText/er/PDF.

4. Utah State Legislature, "H.B. 257 Sex-based Designations for Privacy, Antibullying, and Women's Opportunities," January 30, 2024, https://le.utah.gov/~2024/bills/hbillint/HB0257.htm.

5. Utah State Legislature, "H.B. 257 Sex-based Designations for Privacy, Antibullying, and Women's Opportunities"; see also Amy Beth Hanson, "Utah Joins 10 Other States in Regulating Bathroom Access for Transgender People," Associated Press, January 30, 2024, https://apnews.com/article/utah-transgender-bathroom-access-746d51175ad770623e6f403b426fdc8c.

6. An Act to Amend Section 221.5 of the Education Code, Relating to Pupil Rights, Assembly Bill No. 1266, California State Legislature, August 12, 2013, https://leginfo.legislature.ca.gov/faces/billNavClient.xhtml?bill_id=201320140AB1266.

7. An Act to Amend Section 35292.5 of, and to add Section 17585 to, the Education Code, Relating to School Facilities, California Senate Bill No. 760, September 23, 2023.

8. Hanson, "Utah Joins 10 Other States in Regulating Bathroom Access for Transgender People"; "Sen. Newman Introduces Legislation to Guarantee Access to

All-Gender Restrooms for K-12 Students," press release, February 17, 2023, https://sd29.senate.ca.gov/news/press-release/sen-newman-introduces-legislation-guarantee-access-all-gender-restrooms-k-12.

9. The relationship between space as a technological response and a cultural product is explored in Barbara Penner's "A World of Unmentionable Suffering: Women's Public Conveniences in Victorian London," *Journal of Design History* 14, no. 1 (2001): 35–51.

10. On the development of the department store, see Susan Porter Benson, *Counter Cultures: Saleswomen, Managers, and Customers in American Department Stores, 1890–1940* (Champaign: University of Illinois Press, 1988); William Leach, *Land of Desire: Merchants, Power, and the Rise of a New American Culture* (New York: Pantheon Books, 1993); and Richard W. Longstreth, *The American Department Store Transformed, 1920–1960* (New Haven, CT: Yale University Press, 2010). On the development of ready-made clothing, see Claudia B. Kidwell and Margaret C. Christman, *Suiting Everyone: The Democratization of Clothing in America* (Washington, DC: Smithsonian Institution Press, 1974), 139; and Claudia Brush Kidwell, *Cutting a Fashionable Fit: Dressmakers' Drafting Systems in the United States* (Washington, DC: Smithsonian Institution Press, 1979), 96–98, 137.

11. On the development of public baths, see Marilyn T. Williams, *Washing "The Great Unwashed": Public Baths in Urban America, 1840–1920* (Columbus: Ohio State University Press, 1991).

12. On the development of public restrooms, see Patricia Cooper and Ruth Oldenziel, "Cherished Classifications: Bathrooms and the Construction of Gender/Race on the Pennsylvania Railroad during World War II," *Feminist Studies* 25, no. 1 (Spring 1999): 7–41; Barbara Penner, "A World of Unmentionable Suffering: Women's Public Conveniences in Victorian London," *Journal of Design History* 14, no. 1 (2001): 35–51; and Eliza V. Stoner, "Commodifying Convenience, Cleanliness, and Privacy: American Public Restroom Design since 1851" (master's thesis, University of Delaware, 2006).

13. On the development of physical education in US public schools, see Mabel Lee, *A History of Physical Education and Sports in the U.S.A.* (Hoboken, NJ: Wiley, 1983).

14. "The Boys and Girls," *Herald of Gospel Liberty* 122, no. 1 (January 2, 1930): 10.

15. Chicago Free Bath and Sanitary League, *The Free Bath and Sanitary League Round-up for 1897 on the Free Public Baths of Chicago*, (Chicago, 1897), 24, 52.

16. Elnore Saaranen, interview with author, November 7, 2012; and Dean and Walter Cole, interview with the author, September 21, 2011.

17. People v. Clark and Mills, No. 10481 (New York Court of General Sessions, District 1, 1896); People v. Johnson and Weismuller, No. 6362 (New York Court of General Sessions, District 1, 1896).

18. Judy Attfield, *Wild Things: The Material Culture of Everyday Life* (New York: Berg, 2000); John D'Emilio and Estelle B. Freedman, *Intimate Matters: A History of Sexuality in America* (Chicago: University of Chicago Press, 1988); Nancy Duncan, ed., *BodySpace: Destabilizing Geographies of Gender and Sexuality* (New York: Routledge, 1996); Michel Foucault, *The History of Sexuality* (New York: Random House, 1978); Beverly Gordon, "Intimacy and Objects: A Proxemic Analysis of Gender-Based Response to the Material World," in *The Material Culture of Gender, The Gender of Material Culture*, edited by Katherine Martinex and Kenneth L. Ames (Winterthur,

DE: Winterthur Museum, 1997); Elizabeth Grosz, *Volatile Bodies: Toward a Corporeal Feminism* (Bloomington: Indiana University Press, 1994); John F. Kasson, *Rudeness and Civility: Manners in Nineteenth-Century Urban America* (New York: Hill and Wang, 1990); Angel Kwolek-Folland, "The Domestic Office: Space, Status, and the Gendered Workplace," in *Engendering Business: Men and Women in the Corporate Office, 1870–1930* (Baltimore: Johns Hopkins University Press, 1994); Ali Madanipour, *Public and Private Spaces of the City* (New York: Routledge, 2003); Kathy Peiss, *Cheap Amusements: Working Women and Leisure in Turn-of-the-Century New York* (Philadelphia: Temple University Press, 1986); Ellen Rooney, "A Semiprivate Room," in *Going Public: Feminism and the Shifting Boundaries of the Private Sphere*, edited by Joan Wallach Scott and Debra Keates (Champaign: University of Illinois Press, 2005); and Abigail A. Van Slyck, "The Lady and the Library Loafer: Gender and Public Space in Victorian America," *Winterthur Portfolio* 31, no. 4 (Winter 1996), 221–242.

19. This ideology proposed that the private sphere of the domestic home environment had become increasingly separated from the public realm outside the home over the course of the nineteenth century through the separation of industrial wage work from the home environment. Related to this domestic interpretation of the private is the understanding of the private as gender segregated. The ideology of separate spheres also posited that the domestic, private sphere came to be understood as a decidedly female space, while the public sphere became associated with men, as they typically left the home to enter the public realm of the industrializing nineteenth-century workplace.

20. Particularly relevant to this book are studies of a variety of public spaces, including hotels, railroad cars, and restrooms. A. K. Sandoval-Strausz noted that nineteenth-century hotels sought to create a domestic, private environment by physically separating men and women through gender-segregated entrances, lounges, and dining rooms. In her study of nineteenth-century railroad cars, Amy G. Richter argued that the public space of the railroad car became privatized with the increasing appearance of women and the "domesticated accommodations" women demanded. And Patricia Cooper, Ruth Oldenziel, Barbara Penner, and Eliza Stoner all contended that the notion of the private in public restrooms was based largely on the unquestioned gendering of the spaces. Cooper and Oldenziel recognized female employees' quest to make their restrooms more domestic by adding mirrors and couches for rest. See A. K. Sandoval-Strausz, *Hotel: An American History* (New Haven, CT: Yale University Press, 2007); Amy G. Richter, *Home on the Rails: Women, the Railroad, and the Rise of Public Domesticity* (Chapel Hill: University of North Carolina Press, 2005); Patricia Cooper and Ruth Oldenziel, "Cherished Classifications: Bathrooms and the Construction of Gender/Race on the Pennsylvania Railroad during World War II," *Feminist Studies* 25, no. 1 (Spring 1999): 7–41; Penner, "A World of Unmentionable Suffering"; and Stoner, "Commodifying Convenience, Cleanliness, and Privacy."

21. In *Gay New York*, George Chauncey argued that access to private space helped define middle-class identity at the turn of the twentieth century. Members of the middle class used their larger incomes to purchase increasingly privatized and separate homes in more expensive neighborhoods, while the working class was relegated to decidedly overcrowded tenement housing where privacy was basically nonexistent. Chauncey's descriptions of the ways gay men used new public/private

spaces, particularly restrooms, for their own purposes, provides a starting point for further questions and analysis. And, according to historian Sarah Deutsch, middle-class white women in turn-of-the-twentieth-century Boston were able to move between the private space of their domestic parlor and the public world outside because of their class-based access to privacy. Working-class and African American women were largely unable to access private space from their crowded homes. As noted earlier, Penner discovered that the prospective mixing of classes in women's public restrooms threatened these sites' social construction of privacy. Similarly, Cooper and Oldenziel noted that privacy within women's employee restrooms was predicated on racial segregation. By defining the private as domestic, gender segregated, class- and race-based, or a combination of these, historians argued for a social and cultural understanding of the private. See George Chauncey, *Gay New York: Gender, Urban Culture, and the Making of the Gay Male World, 1890–1940* (New York: Basic Books, 1995); and Sarah Deutsch, *Women and the City: Gender, Space, and Power in Boston, 1870–1940* (New York: Oxford University Press, 2000).

22. In her study of luxury hotel parlors, historian Carolyn Brucken argued that physically separate, gendered spaces were created to protect women's privacy from the intruding male gaze. Ladies' parlors in hotels were considered private because they were visually separate from more public, male spaces in the hotels. Chauncey noted a similar understanding of private space as visually hidden among gay men in turn-of-the-twentieth-century New York. Darkened stairwells, alleys, and secluded parts of city parks could all provide private space for these men as long as they were visually hidden. Moving into the twentieth century, Beth Bailey and David Farber uncovered a similar definition of private space in Hawaiian brothels of the World War II era. Private space within the brothel was created through the formation of separate cubicles divided by very thin walls. Although these divisions provided no auditory or olfactory privacy, they were visually separate and created the private space necessary for the prostitutes and their customers. In her examination of the material culture surrounding early public restrooms, Eliza Stoner noted the importance of visual separation to the private space of the restroom. Stall doors and round-shaped urinals provided physical, visual privacy in the public restroom. See Carolyn E. Brucken, "In the Public Eye: Women and the American Luxury Hotel," *Winterthur Portfolio* 31, no. 4 (Winter 1996): 203–220; Beth L. Bailey and David Farber, *The First Strange Place: Race and Sex in World War II Hawaii* (Baltimore: Johns Hopkins University Press, 1994); Chauncey, *Gay New York,* 179–206; and Stoner, "Commodifying Convenience, Cleanliness, and Privacy," 37.

Chapter 2 • Department Store Fitting Rooms

1. *A Friendly Guide-Book to the Wanamaker Store* (Philadelphia: John Wanamaker, 1915), 17, Hagley Library.

2. Sarah Gordon, *"Make It Yourself": Home Sewing, Gender, and Culture, 1890–1930* (New York: Columbia University Press, 2009), 6.

3. Susan Strasser, *Never Done: A History of American Housework* (New York: Pantheon, 1982), 126, 130.

4. Wendy Gamber, *The Female Economy: The Millinery and Dressmaking Trades, 1860–1930* (Chicago: University of Illinois Press, 1997), 100.

5. "Mrs. Murden's Two Dollar Silk," *Godey's Lady's Book*, no. 48 (April 1854): 320.
6. Gamber, *Female Economy*, 117.
7. Claudia Brush Kidwell, *Cutting a Fashionable Fit: Dressmakers' Drafting Systems in the United States* (Washington, DC: Smithsonian Institution Press, 1979), 2.
8. "Mrs. Murden's Two Dollar Silk," 320.
9. Kidwell, *Cutting a Fashionable Fit*, 18.
10. Janea Whitacre (mistress milliner and mantua-maker, Colonial Williamsburg), interview and demonstration for the author, March 8, 2008.
11. Richard Phillips, *The Book of English Trades, and Library of the Useful Arts* (London: J. Souter, 1821), 224.
12. "Mrs. Murden's Two Dollar Silk," 320.
13. "Mrs. Murden's Two Dollar Silk," 320.
14. "Mrs. Murden's Two Dollar Silk," 322.
15. Susan Porter Benson, *Counter Cultures: Saleswomen, Managers, and Customers in American Department Stores, 1890–1940* (Chicago: University of Illinois Press, 1986), 14–27; Kidwell, *Cutting a Fashionable Fit*, 96–98; Claudia B. Kidwell and Margaret C. Christman, *Suiting Everyone: The Democratization of Clothing in America* (Washington, DC: Smithsonian Institution Press, 1974), 139; William Leach, *Land of Desire: Merchants, Power, and the Rise of a New American Culture* (New York: Random House, 1994), 20; and Traci Parker, *Department Stores and the Black Freedom Movement* (University of North Carolina Press, 2019), 24–25.
16. Rob Schorman, *Selling Style: Clothing and Social Change at the Turn of the Century* (Philadelphia: University of Pennsylvania Press, 2003), 51.
17. "Women's Garment Industry," *Dry Goods Economist* (October 14, 1905): 77; Michael Zakim, *Ready-Made Democracy: A History of Men's Dress in the American Republic, 1760–1860* (Chicago: University of Chicago Press, 2006), 43; Kidwell and Christman, *Suiting Everyone*, 135; and Kidwell, *Cutting a Fashionable Fit*, 94.
18. Kidwell and Christman, *Suiting Everyone*, 139; and Kidwell, *Cutting a Fashionable Fit*, 96–98.
19. "Women's Garment Industry," 77.
20. H. Kristina Haugland, "Blouse," in *The Berg Companion to Fashion*, ed. Valerie Steele (New York: Berg, 2010), 84–85; Schorman, *Selling Style*, 51; and Albert E. Edgar, *How to Advertise a Retail Store, Including Mail Order Advertising and General Advertising: A Complete and Comprehensive Manual for Promoting Publicity* (Columbus, Ohio: The Advertising World, 1913), 274.
21. Kidwell, *Cutting a Fashionable Fit*, 137.
22. "Women's Garment Industry," 77.
23. "Women's Garment Industry," 77.
24. "Sewing at Home Decreases as 'Ready-Mades' Gain Favor," *New York Times*, December 18, 1927.
25. Sue Ainslie Clark and Edith Wyatt, *Making Both Ends Meet: The Income and Outlay of New York Working Girls* (New York: Macmillan Co., 1911), 88–89, 137.
26. Nan Enstad, *Ladies of Labor, Girls of Adventure* (New York: Columbia University Press, 1999), 64–66.
27. Clark and Wyatt, *Making Both Ends Meet*, 7; Benson, *Counter Cultures*, 194; Kathy Peiss, *Cheap Amusements: Working Women and Leisure in Turn-of-the-Century*

New York. (Philadelphia: Temple University Press, 1986), 65; Leach, *Land of Desire,* 78; Enstad, *Ladies of Labor,* 64–65; and Arthur Wiesenberger, *Research Report on the Operation of Bargain Basements* (New York: National Dry Goods Association, 1921), 31.

28. Enstad, *Ladies of Labor,* 64–65.

29. Stuart Blumin, *The Emergence of the Middle Class: Social Experience in the American City, 1760–1900* (New York: Cambridge University Press, 1989), 184–185.

30. Blumin, *Emergence of the Middle Class,* 70.

31. "Ready Made Housekeeping," *Good Housekeeping* (October 1, 1887), 266.

32. Elaine S. Abelson, *When Ladies Go A-Thieving: Middle-Class Shoplifters in the Victorian Department Store* (New York: Oxford University Press, 1989), 5.

33. Michael B. Miller, *The Bon Marche: Bourgeois Culture and the Department Store, 1869–1920* (Princeton, NJ: Princeton University Press, 1981), 26; and Benson, *Counter Cultures,* 14–27.

34. Leach, *Land of Desire,* 20

35. "A Brief History of the Strawbridge & Clothier Store," Strawbridge & Clothier Archive, Accn. 2117, Series V Real Estate Records, Box 33, Hagley Museum and Library, Manuscripts and Archive; and Benson, *Counter Cultures,* 13.

36. Benson, *Counter Cultures,* 13.

37. Benson, *Counter Cultures,* 14.

38. Leach, *Land of Desire,* 112–150; and Benson, *Counter Cultures,* 18–22.

39. "Brief History of the Strawbridge & Clothier Store," 4–8.

40. "Brief History of the Strawbridge & Clothier Store," 8.

41. *Golden Book of the Wanamaker Stores: Jubilee Year, 1861–1911* (Philadelphia: John Wanamaker, Co., 1911), 277.

42. Ralph M. Hower, *History of Macy's New York, 1858–1919* (Cambridge: Harvard University Press, 1943), 323.

43. Benson, *Counter Cultures,* 241.

44. "Brief History of the Strawbridge & Clothier Store," 5.

45. "Ready-Made Garments," *Dry Goods Economist* (January 12, 1901): 52.

46. "Layout for Store 90×100," *Dry Goods Economist* (January 21, 1905): 105; and "Store Arrangement," *Dry Goods Economist* (November 24, 1906): 59.

47. "Store Arrangement," *Dry Goods Economist* (April 23, 1904): 77; and "Store Arrangement," *Dry Goods Economist* (August 26, 1905): 74.

48. "A New Type of Construction," *Dry Goods Economist* (April 27, 1907): 117.

49. "Denver Retailers Are Active," *Dry Goods Economist,* no. 4056 (April 1, 1922): 58.

50. "Simple Elegance the Keynote," *Dry Goods Economist* (April 27, 1907): 91.

51. "Simple Elegance the Keynote," 91.

52. "Simple Elegance the Keynote," 91.

53. "Styles Shown on Michigan Avenue," *Dry Goods Reporter* (April 18, 1914): 51.

54. Simpson Crawford Co., advertisement, *New York Times,* September 23, 1902, 5.

55. See also the Whitman and Adams Co. Store in "New Store for Kennebec Store," *Dry Goods Economist* (April 23, 1904): 77; "Henry Siegel's Boston Store," *Dry Goods Economist* (July 15, 1905): 105; "Baltimore Store Enlarged," *Dry Goods Economist* (July 29, 1905): 8; "Plan for Irregular Store," *Dry Goods Economist* (August 22, 1905): 274; letter to the editor in "Plan for Store 65×138," *Dry Goods Economist* (July 1,

1905): 61; and letter to the editor in "Plan for Store 30×160," *Dry Goods Economist* (September 2, 1905): 67.

56. Edward Hungerford, *The Romance of a Great Store* (New York: Robert M. McBride & Company, 1922), 119.

57. Hungerford, *Romance of a Great Store*, 119.

58. "Store Arrangement," *Dry Goods Economist* (October 24, 1903): 94.

59. "An Irregular-Shaped Store," *Dry Goods Economist* (February 6, 1904): 77.

60. "Store Arrangement," *Dry Goods Economist* (September 30, 1905): 71.

61. "Two Floor Layouts," *Dry Goods Economist* (November 23, 1912): 13.

62. "Second-Floor Plan," *Dry Goods Economist* (February 6, 1904): 77.

63. "Layouts for Retail Stores," *Dry Goods Economist* (January 21, 1905): 103. See also "Store Arrangement," *Dry Goods Economist* (October 17, 1903): 65; and "Plans for Store 132×132," *Dry Goods Economist* (March 23, 1907): 79.

64. "Store Arrangement," *Dry Goods Economist* (February 18, 1905): 241; and "Layout for Store 100×100," *Dry Goods Economist* (February 17, 1906): 249.

65. William Doerflinger, as quoted in "New Fixtures the Factor," *Dry Goods Economist* (June 23, 1906): 7.

66. "Store Arrangement," *Dry Goods Economist* (October 17, 1903): 65.

67. "Plans for Store 120×170," *Dry Goods Economist* (February 2, 1907): 67.

68. "Store Arrangement," *Dry Goods Economist* (October 8, 1904), 83; "Store Arrangement," *Dry Goods Economist* (October 22, 1904): 69; "Store Arrangement," *Dry Goods Economist* (October 29, 1904): 89; "Layouts for Retail Stores," *Dry Goods Economist* (January 21, 1905): 97; "Store Arrangement," *Dry Goods Economist* (December 19, 1903): 47; "Store Arrangement," *Dry Goods Economist* (April 27, 1907): 125; "Store Arrangement," *Dry Goods Economist* (March 5, 1904): 81; and "Plans for Store 60×87," *Dry Goods Economist* (July 7, 1906): 85.

69. "Store Arrangement," *Dry Goods Economist* (February 17, 1906): 249.

70. "Layouts for Retail Stores," *Dry Goods Economist* (January 21, 1905): 97. See also "Store Arrangement," *Dry Goods Economist* (April 14, 1906): 77; and "Plans for Store 84×67," *Dry Goods Economist* (May 19, 1906): 79.

71. "Store Arrangement," *Dry Goods Economist* (December 16, 1905): 51.

72. "Layouts for Retail Stores," *Dry Goods Economist* (January 21, 1905): 103; and "Plans for Store 120×170," *Dry Goods Economist* (February 9, 1907): 75.

73. "Store Arrangement," *Dry Goods Economist* (June 29, 1907): 93. See also "Plan for Store 24×170" *Dry Goods Economist* (July 22, 1905): 94; "Plans for Store 84×67," *Dry Goods Economist* (May 19, 1906): 79; "Plan for Store 38×86," *Dry Goods Economist* (November 3, 1906): 67; "Plans for Store 120×170," *Dry Goods Economist* (February 2, 1907): 67; and "Plan for Store 70×82," *Dry Goods Economist* (March 10, 1906): 67.

74. "Plans for Store 132×132," *Dry Goods Economist* (March 16, 1907): 75.

75. "Seen in the Waiting Room," *Store Chat* 3, no. 1 (January 1909): 12.

76. "A New Dry Goods Store," *The Independent*, October 31, 1878, 17.

77. "Layout for Store 148 ½ × 80," *Dry Goods Economist* (June 18, 1904): 391.

78. " New Home of Dancer-Brogan Co. Provides Ample Facilities," *Dry Goods Economist*, no. 4053 (March 11, 1922): 91.

79. " New Home of Dancer-Brogan Co.," 91.

80. "Seen in the Waiting Room," *Store Chat* 3, no. 1 (January 1909): 12.

81. "Plan for Store 45×140," *Dry Goods Economist* (March 17, 1906): 105.

82. "Store Arrangement," *Dry Goods Economist* (May 12, 1906): 75.

83. Benson, *Counter Cultures*, 78.

84. Wanamaker Co., advertisement, *New York Times*, October 21, 1899, 4; and Wanamaker Co., advertisement, *New York Times*, March 21, 1900, 4.

85. H. O'Neill & Company, advertisement, *New York Times*, October 12, 1903, 2.

86. H. O'Neill & Company, advertisement.

87. "Plans for Store 120×170," *Dry Goods Economist* (February 2, 1907): 63; and "Store Arrangement," *Dry Goods Economist* (July 15, 1905): 91.

88. Benson, *Counter Cultures*, 23.

89. Benson, *Counter Cultures*, 87.

90. "The Fourth Indispensable Element of a Sale," *Store Chat* 5, no. 7 (June 1911): 148.

91. "Fourth Indispensable Element of a Sale," 148.

92. "Who Is This?" *Store Chat* 3, no. 2 (February 1909): 32.

93. "Saleswomen and Salesmen," *Store Chat* 5, no. 2 (January 1911): 27–28.

94. "Personality: Why Some Girls Succeed in Business," *Store Chat* 7, no. 2 (February 1913): 36.

95. "Personality," 36.

96. "A Good Thought from One of Our Store Family," *Store Chat* 5, no. 10 (October 1911): 221.

97. "Store Arrangement," *Dry Goods Economist* (May 11, 1907): 75.

98. Paul H. Nystrom, *Retail Selling and Store Management* (New York: D. Appleton and Company, 1916), 64.

99. Nystrom, *Retail Selling and Store Management*, 64.

100. "Selling and Fitting Corsets," *Store Chat* 9, no. 6 (June 1915): 104.

101. "Store Chat's Service Talks," *Store Chat* 8, no. 10 (October 1914): 245.

102. *Store Chat* 1, no. 6 (June 1906): 9.

103. "What's to Be Done with the Girl Who Has the Manner but Can't Seem to Sell Goods?," *Crockery & Glass Journal* 103, no. 26 (December 30, 1926): 29.

104. "The Boys and Girls," *Herald of Gospel Liberty* 122, no. 1 (January 2, 1930): 10.

105. "Plans for Store 120×160," *Dry Goods Economist* (February 2, 1907): 67.

Chapter 3 • Public Baths

1. "A Boon to the Community: The Big Corporations Are Certainly Not All Soulless," *Copper Country Evening News* (September 16, 1898): 5.

2. Richard L. Bushman and Claudia L. Bushman, "The Early History of Cleanliness in America," *Journal of American History* 74, no. 4 (March, 1988): 1213–1238; Suellen Hoy, *Chasing Dirt: The American Pursuit of Cleanliness* (New York: Oxford University Press, 1995); Marilyn Thornton Williams, *Washing "The Great Unwashed": Public Baths in Urban America, 1840–1920* (Columbus: Ohio State University Press, 1991), 2; Susan Strasser, *Never Done: A History of American Housework* (New York: Pantheon, 1982), 100; Alison K. Hoagland, "Introducing the Bathroom: Space and Change in Working-Class Houses," *Buildings & Landscapes* 18, no. 2 (Fall 2011): 18; Amy L. Fairchild, Ronald Bayer, James Keith Colgrove, and Daniel Wolfe, *Searching Eyes: Privacy, the State, and Disease Surveillance in America* (Oakland: University of

California Press, 2007); Oliver J. T. Harris and John Robb, "Multiple Ontologies and the Problem of the Body in History," *American Anthropologist*, n.s, 114, no. 4 (December 2012): 668–679.

3. Williams, *Washing "The Great Unwashed,"* 2.

4. Strasser, *Never Done*, 90; and Hoagland, "Introducing the Bathroom," 18.

5. Strasser, *Never Done*, 90; Hoagland, "Introducing the Bathroom," 18; and Dean and Walter Cole, interview with author, September 21, 2011.

6. Bruce Norden, interviewed by Jo Urion, January 14, 2003, Oral History Collection, Keweenaw National Historical Park.

7. Bertha H. Smith, "The Public Bath," *The Outlook* 66, no. 2 (September 8, 1900): 567.

8. Larry Lankton, *Cradle to Grave: Life, Work, and Death at the Lake Superior Copper Mines* (New York: Oxford University Press, 1991), 156.

9. Department of Commerce and Labor, Bureau of the Census, *Thirteenth Census of the United States Taken in the Year 1910: Statistics for Michigan* (Washington, DC: Government Printing Office, 1913), 606, https://www2.census.gov/library/publications/decennial/1910/abstract/supplement-mi.pdf; Lankton, *Cradle to Grave*, 213; and Hoagland, "Introducing the Bathroom," 19.

10. Hoagland, "Introducing the Bathroom," 19.

11. Elnore Saaranen, interview with author, November 7, 2012; and Hoagland, "Introducing the Bathroom," 19.

12. Elnore Saaranen, interview with author, November 7, 2012.

13. Pekka Leimu, "The Finnish Sauna and Its Finnishness," in *Water Leisure and Culture: European Historical Perspectives*, ed. Susan C. Anderson and Bruce H. Tabb (New York: Berg, 2002), 73.

14. Leimu, "Finnish Sauna and Its Finnishness," 79–80.

15. *The Fleischman Baths: Bryant Park Building, Forty-second St. & Sixth Avenue, New York City* (New York: Joseph Fleischman, 1908).

16. "Modern Sanitation and Modern Plumbing," *The Outlook* (June 6, 1917): 236.

17. Dean and Walter Cole, interview with author, September 21, 2011.

18. Hoagland, "Introducing the Bathroom," 19–20.

19. "Labor Conditions at Copper Range," *Engineering and Mining Journal* 94, no. 26 (December 28, 1912): 1232.

20. Bushman and Bushman, "Early History of Cleanliness in America," 1215.

21. Martin V. Melosi, *The Sanitary City: Environmental Services in Urban America from Colonial Times to the Present* (Pittsburgh: University of Pittsburgh Press, 2008), 50–51; Ellen Lupton and J. Abbott Miller, *The Bathroom, the Kitchen and the Aesthetics of Waste* (New York: Kiosk, 1992), 22–23; and Hoy, *Chasing Dirt*, 14.

22. Hoagland, "Introducing the Bathroom," 15; Merritt Ierley, *The Comforts of Home: The American Home and the Evolution of Modern Convenience* (New York: Clarkson Potter, 1999), 141–142; and Lupton and Miller, *Bathroom*, 25.

23. Strasser, *Never Done*, 97, 100–103; Hoagland, "Introducing the Bathroom," 16; and Ierley, *Comforts of Home*, 10.

24. Hoagland, "Introducing the Bathroom," 16–17.

25. Alison K. Hoagland, *Mine Towns: Buildings for Workers in Michigan's Copper Country* (Minneapolis: University of Minnesota Press, 2010), 149 and Hoagland, "Introducing the Bathroom," 24–25.

26. New York (NY) Mayor's Committee on Public Baths and Public Comfort Stations, *Report on Public Baths and Public Comfort Stations* (New York: Mayor's Committee, 1897), 11.

27. Bushman and Bushman, "Early History of Cleanliness in America," 1231–1232; Strasser, *Never Done*, 100; and Hoagland, "Introducing the Bathroom," 18.

28. Bushman and Bushman, "Early History of Cleanliness in America," 1228; Hoy, *Chasing Dirt*, 16; and Williams, *Washing "The Great Unwashed,"* 2.

29. Bushman and Bushman, "The Early History of Cleanliness in America," 1228.

30. Williams, *Washing "The Great Unwashed,"* 2–3; and Hoagland, *Mine Towns*, 180–186.

31. "The Story of a Failure," *The Outlook* (December 13, 1913): 806.

32. William Paul Gerhard, "Public Bath Houses and Swimming Pools," *American City* 11, no. 5 (November 1914): 358.

33. Stanley H. Howe, *History and Condition and Needs of Public Baths in Manhattan*, New York Association for Improving the Condition of the Poor, Publication 71 (ca. 1912), 12.

34. Smith, "Public Bath," 573.

35. Howe, *History and Condition and Needs of Public Baths in Manhattan*, 18.

36. Smith, "Public Bath," 575.

37. Gerhard, "Public Bath Houses and Swimming Pools," 360, 366.

38. Smith, "Public Bath," 575; and Donald B. Armstrong, "Public Laundries in America," *American City* 9, no. 6 (December 1913): 528.

39. "The Business Government of Cities," *The Outlook* 52, no. 7 (August 17, 1895): 270.

40. "Settlement Work," *The Outlook* 73, no. 15 (April 11, 1903): 859.

41. Hoagland, *Mine Towns*, 180–183.

42. Melosi, *Sanitary City*, 5; and Tomes, *Gospel of Germs*, 6.

43. Tomes, *Gospel of Germs*, 6.

44. "Municipal Free Baths in New York," *Medical News* 70, no. 12 (March 20, 1897): 372.

45. "Municipal Free Baths in New York," 372.

46. Chicago Free Bath and Sanitary League, *The Free Bath and Sanitary League Round-up for 1897 on the Free Public Baths of Chicago* (Chicago, 1897), 16.

47. "Municipal Bathing Establishments," *Scientific American* 80, no. 24 (June 17, 1899): 388–389.

48. Everett B. Mero, "How Public Gymnasiums and Baths Help to Make Good Citizens," *American City* 1, no. 1 (September 1909): 70.

49. Mero, "How Public Gymnasiums and Baths Help," 70.

50. Smith, "Public Bath," 573.

51. Mero, "How Public Gymnasiums and Baths Help," 70.

52. Josiah Quincy, "Valedictory Message," Boston City Document 170 (December 30, 1899), 45.

53. Quoted in Smith, "Public Bath," 576.

54. Smith, "Public Bath," 573.

55. William J. Cole, *Free Municipal Baths in Boston* (Boston: Boston Municipal Printing Office, 1899), 16.

56. Hoagland, *Mine Towns*, 183; and US Senate, *Strike in the Copper Mining District of Michigan*, 63rd Cong., 2nd sess., 1914, S. Doc. 381: 133.
57. Hoagland, "Introducing the Bathroom," 16, 24.
58. *Free Bath and Sanitary League Round-up for 1897*, 16.
59. Thomas J. Schlereth, *Victorian America: Transformations in Everyday Life, 1876–1915* (New York: HarperCollins, 1991), 8.
60. Campbell J. Gibson and Emily Lennon, *Tech Paper 29: Table 19. Nativity of the Population for the 50 Largest Urban Places: 1870 to 1990* (Washington, DC: US Bureau of the Census, Population Division, February 1999).
61. Albert Wilhem, "The Public Bath as an Americanizer," *Modern Sanitation* 10, no. 7 (July 1913): 270.
62. Smith, "Public Bath," 576.
63. Smith, "Public Bath," 576.
64. Wilhelm, "Public Bath as an Americanizer," 271.
65. Wilhelm, "Public Bath as an Americanizer," 271.
66. Abigail A. Van Slyck, "The Lady and the Library Loafer: Gender and Public Space in Victorian America," *Winterthur Portfolio* 31, no. 4 (Winter 1996): 221–242.
67. See John Duffy, *A History of Public Health in New York City, 1866–1966* (New York: Russell Sage Foundation, 1974); Harold Donaldson Eberlein, "When Society First Took a Bath," *Pennsylvania Magazine of History and Biography* 67 (January 1943): 30–48; David Glassberg, "The Design of Reform: The Public Bath Movement in America," *American Studies* 20, no. 2 (1979): 5–21; Hoy, *Chasing Dirt*; Andrea Renner, "A Nation That Bathes Together: Finding Class in Turn-of-the-Century New York Public Baths" (master's thesis, University of Delaware, 2005); Jacqueline S. Wilkie, "Submerged in Sensuality: Technology and Perceptions of Bathing," *Journal of Social History* 19 (1986): 649–664; Williams, *Washing "The Great Unwashed"*; Lawrence Wright, *Clean and Decent: The Fascinating History of the Bathroom and the Water Closet* (London: Routledge & Kegan Paul, 1960).
68. Williams, *Washing "The Great Unwashed,"* 19.
69. New York (NY) Mayor's Committee on Public Baths and Public Comfort Stations, *Report on Public Baths and Public Comfort Stations*, 182.
70. *Free Bath and Sanitary League Round-up for 1897*, 54.
71. *Public Baths Under the Supervision of the President of the Borough of Manhattan* (New York: Borough of Manhattan, Public Works Department, 1914).
72. "Rules of the Calumet Baths of the Calumet & Hecla Mining Company," December 1911, 2–4, Keweenaw National Historic Park.
73. *Free Bath and Sanitary League Round-up for 1897*, 56.
74. Gerhard, "Public Bath Houses and Swimming Pools," 366; and Hoagland, *Mine Towns*, 183.
75. Gerhard, "Public Bath Houses and Swimming Pools," 366.
76. Bruce Norden, interviewed by Jo Urion, January 14, 2003, Oral History Collection, Keweenaw National Historical Park.
77. Howe, *History and Condition and Needs of Public Baths in Manhattan*, 20.
78. Gerhard, "Public Bath Houses and Swimming Pools," 358; and Smith, "Public Bath," 571.
79. Gerhard, "Public Bath Houses and Swimming Pools," 364–365.

80. "Rules of the Calumet Baths," 1.

81. "New Bathhouse Is Ready," *Daily Mining Gazette*, December 10, 1911, 10.

82. William Todd to Charles Lawton, March 17, 1916, MS-001, Box 366, Folder 9, Michigan Technological University Archives.

83. Gerhard, "Public Bath Houses and Swimming Pools," 366.

84. Gerhard, "Public Bath Houses and Swimming Pools," 366.

85. "The Proper Methods of Bathing," *American Medicine* II, no. 10 (September 7, 1901): 354.

86. "Proper Methods of Bathing," 354.

87. "Proper Methods of Bathing," 354.

88. *The Outlook* 53, no. 21 (May 23, 1896), 926.

89. Calumet Bath Reports, MS-002, Box 212, Folder 33, Michigan Technological University Archives

90. Dean Cole and Walter Cole, interview with author, September 21, 2011.

91. "Public Baths," *The Outlook* 52, no. 14 (October 5, 1895): 545.

92. "Public Baths," 545.

93. "New Bathhouse Is Ready," 10.

94. Calumet Bath Reports.

95. John and Evelyn Buckett, interviewed by Jo Urion, March 27, 2002, Oral History Collection, Keweenaw National Historical Park.

96. Bruce Norden, interviewed by Jo Urion, January 14, 2003, Oral History Collection, Keweenaw National Historical Park.

97. Calumet Bath Reports.

98. Lucy Cleveland, "The Public Baths of Chicago," *Modern Sanitation* 5, no. 5 (October 1908): 8.

99. Cleveland, "Public Baths of Chicago," 9.

100. *Free Bath and Sanitary League Round-up for 1897*, 24.

101. *Free Bath and Sanitary League Round-up for 1897*, 52.

102. "William N. Walker, Respondent v. City of Buffalo, Appellant," *Cases Decided in the Courts of Record of the State of New York* (J. B. Lyon Company: Albany, 1919), 640–644; and "Hoffman v. Roman Baths," *New York Supplement* (St. Paul, MN: West Publishing Company, 1915), 563–564.

103. *Free Bath and Sanitary League Round-up for 1897*, 54.

104. *Free Bath and Sanitary League Round-up for 1897*, 52.

105. *Free Bath and Sanitary League Round-up for 1897*, 24.

Chapter 4 • *Creating Privacy in Public*

1. New York (NY) Mayor's Committee on Public Baths and Public Comfort Stations, *Report on Public Baths and Public Comfort Stations* (New York: Mayor's Committee, 1897), 174.

2. "The Public Comfort Station in America," *Engineering Review* 22, no. 5 (May 1912): 35–36.

3. Dr. Woods Hutchinson, quoted in "Public Comfort Stations for Chicago," *Bulletin of the Department of Public Welfare, City of Chicago* 1, no. 3 (October 1916): 15.

4. "Public Comfort Stations," *Sanitary Pottery* 6, no. 9 (January 1915): 12.

5. *Report on Public Baths and Public Comfort Stations*, 142.

6. Louise de Koven Bowen, *The Public Dance Halls of Chicago* (Chicago: Juvenile Protective Association of Chicago, 1917), 7.

7. "Another Need Emphasized by Prohibition," *American Architect* 115, no. 2262 (April 30, 1919): 620.

8. Women's City Club of New York, *Comfort Stations of New York City: Today and Tomorrow* (New York: Women's City Club of New York, 1932), 46.

9. Women's City Club of New York, *Comfort Stations of New York City*, 16.

10. "Public Comfort Stations for Chicago," 8.

11. *Philadelphia Medical Times* 3, no. 51 (September 20, 1873): 808.

12. "Mayor's Black Book," *New York Daily Times*, January 24, 1855, 6.

13. "Public Urinals," *Medical and Surgical Reporter* 17, no. 13 (September 28, 1867): 273.

14. "Public Urinals," 273.

15. *Philadelphia Medical Times* 5, no. 50 (September 11, 1875): 792.

16. "Public Urinals," 273.

17. Barbara Penner, "A World of Unmentionable Suffering: Women's Public Conveniences in Victorian London," *Journal of Design History* 14, no. 1 (2001): 38.

18. Penner, "A World of Unmentionable Suffering," 38.

19. Penner, "A World of Unmentionable Suffering," 38–39.

20. William Paul Gerhard, "Public Comfort Stations: Their Location, Plan, Construction, Equipment and Care," *American City* 14, no. 5 (May 1916): 449.

21. Gerhard, "Public Comfort Stations," 449.

22. Women's City Club of New York, *Comfort Stations of New York City*, 35.

23. Gerhard, "Public Comfort Stations," 451.

24. Gerhard, "Public Comfort Stations," 457.

25. Gerhard, "Public Comfort Stations," 454.

26. New York (NY) Mayor's Committee on Public Baths and Public Comfort Stations, *Report on Public Baths and Public Comfort Stations*, 176.

27. Jon Webster to Charles H. T. Collis, July 8, 1896, New York, Map Division, New York Public Library.

28. George W. Simons Jr., "More Public Convenience Stations Needed," *American City* 23, no. 5 (November 1920): 474.

29. "Planning Public Comfort Stations," *Sanitary Pottery* 6, no. 12 (April 1915): 13.

30. Juster Collom, "Odds and Ends," *Domestic Engineering* 95, no. 1 (April 2, 1921): 12.

31. "Public Comfort Stations for Chicago," 24.

32. Fredrick L. Ford, "Monograph on Public Comfort Stations," in *Fourth Annual Report of the Commission on the City Plan to the Mayor and Court of Common Council, City of Hartford, Connecticut* (Hartford: Hartford Press, 1911): 22.

33. Collom, "Odds and Ends," 12.

34. Trenton Potteries Co., "Silent Siwelclo" advertisement, *Sanitary Pottery* 6, no. 4 (August 1914): 16.

35. "Public Comfort Station in Newark, N.J.," *Building Age* (May 1, 1910): 219; Gerhard, "Public Comfort Stations," 453.

36. A. L. H. Street, "All Municipalities in Wisconsin Must Provide Comfort Stations," *American City* 21, no. 3 (September 1919): 279.

37. "The Need for Building Public Convenience Stations," *American Architect* 17, no. 2321 (June 16, 1920): 775; Gerhard, "Public Comfort Stations," 452.

38. Samuel Goodwin Gant, *Constipation and Intestinal Obstruction* (Philadelphia: W. B. Saunders Company, 1909), 60.

39. Ford, "Monograph on Public Comfort Stations," 46.

40. Ford, "Monograph on Public Comfort Stations," 25.

41. "Public Comfort Stations," *Sanitary Pottery* 6, no. 9 (January 1915): 11.

42. "Public Comfort Stations," *Sanitary Pottery* 6, no. 9 (January 1915): 11.

43. Women's City Club of New York, *Comfort Stations of New York City*, 46.

44. "Planning Public Comfort Stations," *Sanitary Pottery* 6, no. 12 (April 1915): 13.

45. "Public Comfort Station in Newark, N.J.," 219.

46. Gerhard, "Public Comfort Stations," 452.

47. Gerhard, "Public Comfort Stations," 454.

48. *Mott's Plumbing Catalogue "A"* (New York: J. L. Mott Iron Works, 1908), 400.

49. *Mott's Plumbing Catalogue "A,"* 400.

50. "Dallas Public Comfort Station: A Comfort Station in Which Provisions Are Made for Two Races," *American Architect and the Architectural Review* 121, no. 2389 (May 15, 1922): 231.

51. "Dallas Public Comfort Station," 231.

52. "Improving the Public Square in Paris, Texas," *American City* 5, no. 2 (August 1911): 78–81.

53. Ford, "Monograph on Public Comfort Stations," 45.

54. Ford, "Monograph on Public Comfort Stations," 45.

55. Quoted in "Public Comfort Stations for Chicago," 15.

56. "Public Comfort Stations," *Sanitary Pottery* 6, no. 9 (January 1915): 12.

57. Gerhard, "Public Comfort Stations," 453–454.

58. Gerhard, "Public Comfort Stations," 454; and New York (NY) Mayor's Committee on Public Baths and Public Comfort Stations, *Report on Public Baths and Public Comfort Stations*, 180.

59. Simons, "More Public Convenience Stations Needed," 473.

60. Donald B. Armstrong, "Public Comfort Stations: Their Economy and Sanitation," *American City* 11, no. 2 (August 1914): 102.

61. *Mott's Plumbing Catalogue "A,"* 404.

62. Gerhard, "Public Comfort Stations," 455.

63. Simons, "More Public Convenience Stations Needed," 472.

64. New York (NY) Mayor's Committee on Public Baths and Public Comfort Stations, *Report on Public Baths and Public Comfort Stations*, 142.

65. "Public Comfort Stations for Chicago," 8.

66. New York (NY) Mayor's Committee on Public Baths and Public Comfort Stations, *Report on Public Baths and Public Comfort Stations*, 143.

67. Street, "All Municipalities in Wisconsin Must Provide Comfort Stations," 279.

68. Gerhard, "Public Comfort Stations," 455; and J. J. Cosgrove, *Standards for Public Comfort Stations* (New York: Public Comfort Station Bureau, 1916).

69. New York (NY) Mayor's Committee on Public Baths and Public Comfort Stations, *Report on Public Baths and Public Comfort Stations*, 166.

70. "What It Costs to Maintain Public Comfort Stations," *Domestic Engineering* 95, no. 1 (April 2, 1921): 11.

71. Women's City Club of New York, *Comfort Stations of New York City*, 30.

72. Women's City Club of New York, *Comfort Stations of New York City*, 18.

73. George Chauncey, "'Privacy Could Only Be Had in Public': Gay Uses of the Streets," in *Stud: Architectures of Masculinity*, edited by Joel Sanders (Princeton, NJ: Princeton Architectural Press, 1996), 225–226.

74. People v. Clark and Mills, no. 10481 (New York Court of General Sessions, District 1, 1896).

75. People v. Clark and Mills.

76. People v. Johnson and Weismuller, no. 6362 (New York Court of General Sessions, District 1, 1896).

77. J. J. Cosgrove, *Standards for Public Comfort Stations*.

78. Women's City Club of New York, *Comfort Stations of New York City*, 45.

79. Gerhard, "Public Comfort Stations," 456.

80. Gerhard, "Public Comfort Stations," 456.

81. Gerhard, "Public Comfort Stations," 456.

82. New York (NY) Mayor's Committee on Public Baths and Public Comfort Stations, *Report on Public Baths and Public Comfort Stations*, 180; and Women's City Club of New York, *Comfort Stations of New York City*, 45.

83. Women's City Club of New York, *Comfort Stations of New York City*, 18.

84. Ford, "Monograph on Public Comfort Stations," 66.

85. Ford, "Monograph on Public Comfort Stations," 66.

86. Ford, "Monograph on Public Comfort Stations," 69.

87. Ford, "Monograph on Public Comfort Stations," 68.

Chapter 5 • *Learning Privacy*

1. "Painesdale High School an Efficient Institution," *Daily Mining Gazette*, March 21, 1912, 2.

2. Scholarship on the history of physical education in public schools is somewhat limited. Scholars of public school history have focused on the development of the system during the Progressive era but tend to mention the development of physical education programs only in passing. See Lawrence A. Cremin's *The Transformation of the School: Progressivism in American Education, 1876–1957* (New York: Vintage Books, 1961) and David Nasaw's *Schooled to Order: A Social History of Public Schooling in the United States* (Oxford: Oxford University Press, 1979). Other scholars who have directly addressed the history of physical education in public schools have focused on pedagogy and the formal institutions surrounding the development of physical education programs. See Mabel Lee, *A History of Physical Education and Sports in the U.S.A.* (Hoboken, NJ: Wiley, 1983). Past scholarship on public schools and physical education does not address the development of physical spaces within these schools.

3. Lee, *A History of Physical Education*, 79.

4. William J. Reese, *The Origins of the American High School* (Hartford, CT: Yale University Press, 1999), 7; and Lee, *A History of Physical Education*, 79.

5. "Getting the Immigrant Child to School," *American City* 13, no. 4 (October 1915): 323.

6. "Getting the Immigrant Child to School," 323.

7. William J. Reese, *America's Public Schools: From the Common School to "No Child Left Behind"* (Baltimore: Johns Hopkins University Press, 2011), 119.

8. Reese, *America's Public Schools*, 119.

9. Stephen Provasnik, "Judicial Activism and the Origins of Parental Choice: The Court's Role in the Institutionalization of Compulsory Education in the United States, 1891-1925," *History of Education Quarterly* 46, no. 3 (Fall 2006): 312.

10. Johann N. Neem, *Democracy's Schools: The Rise of Public Education in America* (Baltimore: Johns Hopkins University Press, 2017), 119-120.

11. Neem, *Democracy's Schools*, 119-120; and G. Stanley Hall, "The Physiology and Psychology of Adolescence," reprinted in *Childhood in America* (New York: New York University Press, 2000), 139-141.

12. Neem, *Democracy's Schools*, 119.

13. Alison K. Hoagland, *Mine Towns: Buildings for Workers in Michigan's Copper Country* (Minneapolis: University of Minnesota Press, 2010), 196.

14. Hoagland, *Mine Towns*, 196; and Claude T. Rice, "Labor Conditions at Copper Range," *Engineering and Mining Journal* 94, no. 26 (December 28, 1912): 1229.

15. Hoagland, *Mine Towns*, 197-198.

16. "Education: Partners," *Time*, December 3, 1945, 74.

17. Linda J. Tomko, *Dancing Class: Gender, Ethnicity, and Social Divides in American Dance, 1890-1920* (Bloomington: Indiana University Press, 1999), 10.

18. Edward Dana Caulkins, "Universal Physical Education for Children," *American City* 24, no. 6 (June 1921): 587.

19. Caulkins, "Universal Physical Education for Children," 587.

20. "Hygiene in the Schools," *The Independent* 38, no. 1974 (September 30, 1886): 8.

21. Dean Cole, discussion with author, September 21, 2011.

22. John Donald Gustav-Wrathall, *Take the Young Stranger by the Hand: Same-Sex Relations and the YMCA* (Chicago: University of Chicago Press, 1998), 29; and Tomko, *Dancing Class*, 17.

23. E. Bosworth McCready, "Mental and Physical Hygiene of Children," *Alienist and Neurologist* 38, no. 4 (November 1, 1917): 428.

24. W. M. Conant, "The Educational Aspects of College Athletics," *Boston Medical and Surgical Journal* (October 18, 1894), reprinted in Roberta J. Park, "Physiologists, Physicians, and Physical Educators: Nineteenth Century Biology and Exercise, 'Hygienic' and 'Educative,'" in "Sport, Exercise, and American Medicine," special issue, *Journal of Sport History* 14, no. 1 (Spring 1987): 29.

25. "Baths, Breakfast and Fresh Air in a Philadelphia School," *American City* 10, no. 2 (February 1914): 153.

26. Tomko, *Dancing Class*, 17.

27. Harry R. Allen, "Gymnasiums in Public Schools," *American City* 7, no. 4 (October 1912): 335.

28. Florence Harvey Richards, *Hygiene for Girls* (Boston: D.C. Heath & Co., 1913), 144.

29. Lee, *A History of Physical Education*, 166, 174-175.

30. Marilyn T. Williams, *Washing "The Great Unwashed": Public Baths in Urban America, 1840-1920* (Columbus: Ohio State University Press, 1991), 3.

31. Williams, *Washing "The Great Unwashed,"* 25.

32. Albert Wilhelm, "The Public Bath as an Americanizer," *Modern Sanitation* 10, no. 7 (July 1913): 271.

33. Wilhelm, "The Public Bath as an Americanizer," 272.

34. "Health Instruction," *American City* 15, no. 4 (October 1916): 426.

35. Robert F. G. Kelley, "The Public School Baths of Baltimore, Md.," *American City* 24, no. 5 (May 1921): 511.

36. Quoted in Robert F. Kelley, "Public School Baths," *Mind and Body* 28, no. 297 (April 1921): 509.

37. Henry Hale, "Bathing in the Public Schools," *Modern Sanitation* 10, no. 1 (January 1913): 32.

38. Howe, *History and Condition and Needs of Public Baths in Manhattan*, 21.

39. Dean Cole and Walter Cole, interview with author, September 21, 2011; and Elnore Saaranen, interview with author, November 7, 2012.

40. Dean Cole and Walter Cole, interview with author, September 21, 2011.

41. Hoagland, *Mine Towns*, 142.

42. Mayor's Committee on Public Baths and Comfort Stations, *Report on Public Baths and Public Comfort Stations* (New York: The Mayor's Committee, 1897), 59

43. Mayor's Committee, *Report on Public Baths and Public Comfort Stations*, 59.

44. Hale, "Bathing in the Public Schools," 19.

45. Hale, "Bathing in the Public Schools," 19.

46. "A Plea for Rain-Baths in the Public Schools," *American Architect and Building News* 69, no. 1281 (July 14, 1900): 11; and Hale, "Bathing in the Public Schools," 19.

47. A. G. Young, "Bathing and the Different Forms of Baths," quoted in "A Plea for Rain-Baths in the Public Schools," 12.

48. "A Plea for Rain-Baths in the Public Schools," 11.

49. "A Plea for Rain-Baths in the Public Schools," 11.

50. Chicago Free Bath and Sanitary League, *The Free Bath and Sanitary League Round-up for 1897 on the Free Public Baths of Chicago* (Chicago, 1897), 40–41.

51. *Free Bath and Sanitary League Round-up for 1897*, 40–41.

52. Hale, "Bathing in the Public Schools," 18.

53. Hale, "Bathing in the Public Schools," 18.

54. *Free Bath and Sanitary League Round-up for 1897*, 40–41.

55. *Free Bath and Sanitary League Round-up for 1897*, 40–41.

56. "A Plea for Rain-Baths in the Public Schools," 12.

57. "Hygiene in the Schools," 9.

58. Dean Cole, discussion with author, September 21, 2011.

59. Kelley, "Public School Baths of Baltimore, Md.," 512.

60. "School House Baths," *Cincinnati Lancet and Clinic* 44 (January 13, 1900): 31.

61. C. E. Dobbin, "Swimming Pools for Public Schools," *American Architect* 115, no. 2253 (February 26, 1919): 328; and Kelley, "Public School Baths of Baltimore, Md.," 512.

62. Elnore Saaranen, interview with author, November 7, 2012; and Dean Cole and Walter Cole, interview with author, September 21, 2011.

63. *Free Bath and Sanitary League Round-up for 1897*, 40–41.

64. *Free Bath and Sanitary League Round-up for 1897*, 40–41.

65. *Free Bath and Sanitary League Round-up for 1897*, 40–41.

66. For example, H. A. Jones, "The Status of Equipment in Athletic, Health, and Physical-Education Departments of One Hundred High Schools in the United States," *School Review* 38, no. 1 (January 1930): 57; and Messrs. Brainerd and Leeds, "School

Remodeling or Enlargement," *American Architect* 110, no. 2127 (September 27, 1916): 190.

67. Allison & Allison, Architects, "Merced Union High School Group," *American Architect* 113, no. 2196 (January 23, 1918): 92.

68. John William Gregg, "The Landscape Development of School Grounds," *American City* 14, no. 1 (January 1916): 38; James O. Betelle, "Essentials of High School Planning," *American Architect* 108, no. 2073 (September 15, 1915): 161; Jones, "The Status of Equipment," 57; and Allen, "Gymnasiums in Public Schools," 338.

69. Shand & Eastman, "Plans for School Building District No. 1 Calumet, MI," 1903, Keweenaw National Historic Park; and John J. Donovan, "The Public School Buildings of Oakland, California," *American Architect* 107, no. 2057 (May 26, 1915): 327.

70. Dean Cole, interview with author, September 21, 2011; Everett B. Mero, "How to Start a Municipal Gymnasium," *American City* 2, no. 1 (January 1910): 27; and Betelle, "Essentials of High School Planning," 164.

71. A. D. F. Hamlin, "Consideration in School House Design, Part 2," *American Architect* 96, no. 1770 (November 24, 1909): 228.

72. Dean Cole, interview with author, September 21, 2011.

73. Elnore Saaranen, interview with author, November 7, 2012.

74. Dean Cole and Walter Cole, interview with author, September 21, 2011.

75. "Educational News and Editorial Comment," *School Review* 38, no. 9 (November 1930): 648; and Walter Cole, interview with author, September 21, 2011.

76. "A Plea for Rain-Baths in the Public Schools," 20.

77. Dobbin, "Swimming Pools for Public Schools," 319.

78. Hale, "Bathing in the Public Schools," 32.

79. Hale, "Bathing in the Public Schools," 32.

80. John D. Chubb, "Basement Floor Plan Footings & Details Additions & Alterations to High School Building" (Painesdale, MI), July 3, 1933, and extant Washington Middle School, Calumet, MI.

81. William P. Gerhard, as quoted in Henry Hale, "Bathing in the Public Schools," *Modern Sanitation* 10, no. 1 (January 1913): 34.

82. Dobbin, "Swimming Pools for Public Schools," 320.

83. "Painesdale High School an Efficient Institution," 2.

84. Elnore Saaranen, interview with author, November 7, 2012.

85. Dean Cole and Walter Cole, interview with author, September 21, 2011.

86. "Educational News and Editorial Comment," 648.

87. Kelley, "Public School Baths of Baltimore, Md.," 511.

88. A. D. F. Hamlin, "Consideration in School House Design, Part 1," *American Architect* 96, no. 1769 (November 17, 1909): 193.

89. Earl H. Taylor, "What Is Being Done for Children in Winfield, Kans.," *American City* 13, no. 5 (November 1915): 383; Dean Cole, interview with author, September 21, 2011; and Kelley, "Public School Baths of Baltimore, Md.," 511.

90. Elnore Saaranen, interview with author, November 7, 2012.

INDEX

Note: Illustrations are indicated by page numbers in *italics*.

adolescence, 90, 92, 103, 110–11. *See also* children
African Americans, 118n21. *See also* racial segregation
Americanization, 94. *See also* citizenship
attendants, in comfort stations, 64–65, 75, 86–87

Bailey, Beth, 118n22
bathhouses, private, 38, 40–42, *41*
bathing: Americanization and, 94; bodies and, 44–46; class and, 37–38, 42–44; ethnically diverse traditions of, 39–40; exclusion and, 38–39, 42, 44, 46, 51, 62; Finnish traditions for, 39–40; gender and, 39–40, 42; in home, 38–39, 42–46, *43*, *45*; industrial, 41–42, *43*; locker rooms and, 96–97; privacy and, 38–39, 44–46; traditional techniques for, 38–42
bathrooms: for bathing in home, 42–46, *43*, *45*. *See also* restrooms, public
baths, public, 5–6; class and, 36–38, 46–52, 58, 60–61, 112–13; design of, 52–57, *53–57*; "floating," 52; gender and, 51–57, 60; hygiene and, 46–52, 58–60; immigrants and, 50–51; as movement, 46–52; privacy and, 51–53, 57–58; public health and, 48–49; showers in, 56–57, *57*; social issues and, 49; surveillance in, 37, 42, 51, 60–62
Benson, Susan Porter, 16
body(ies): bathing and, 38–39, 44–46; dressmaking and, 12; female, 3; fitting rooms and, 9; privacy and, 37; protection of, 3; taboos around, 4
Brucken, Carolyn, 118n22
Buckett, John, 61

California, 1
Chauncey, George, 85, 117n21
children: in adolescence, 92, 129n2; bathing of, in home, 38; cleanliness and, 94–95, 97–99, 110–11; in comfort stations, 75; health of, 99; locker rooms and, 90, 96–97; physical education and, 92–93; at public baths, 36, 54; in public restrooms, 2, 75; public schooling and, 89; urbanization and, 93–94
citizenship, 47–48, 91. *See also* Americanization
class: bathing and, 37–38, 42–44; bathrooms and, 44; clothing and, 14–15; comfort stations and, 75–82; dressmaking and, 11; fitting rooms and, 6, 25–26, 34–35; gender and, 6; locker rooms and, 90–91, 110; physical education and, 94–95; privacy and, 3–5, 26, 90, 113, 117n21; public baths and, 36–38, 46–52, 58, 60–61, 112–13; public toileting and, 66–67
cleanliness, 36–37, 46, 83, 94–95, 97–99, 110–11. *See also* bathing; hygiene
clothing: class and, 14–15; custom-made, 10–13; department stores and, 15–20, *16–17*, *19*; ready-made, 13–15, 20. *See also* fitting rooms
Cole, Dean, 38, 93, 95, 98, 110

Index

Cole, Walter, 42, 95, 108, 110
comfort stations, *64*; attendants in, 64–65, 75, 86–87; class and, 75–82; defined, 68; emergence of, 63, 68; in Europe, 71–72; gay men and, 85–86; gender and, 63–64, 73–75; misuse of, 84–86; morality and, 83–84; physical construction of, 69–73, *70–72*, 75–82; privacy and, 63–64, 69–70, 72–73, 75–82; public health and, 82–83; racial segregation of, 78–82, *79*; social construction in, 73–75, 78–82, *79*; sounds in, 72–73; surveillance in, 86–87; transgression in, 84–86. *See also* restrooms, public
consumer culture, 15
Cooper, Patricia, 117n20
Counter Cultures: Saleswomen, Managers, and Customers in American Department Stores, 1890–1940 (Benson), 16
COVID-19 pandemic, 114

decorum, 4–5
department stores, 4, 15–20, *16–17, 19*, 26–29, 66. *See also* fitting rooms
domestic aspect, of privacy, 10–11, 117n19
dressing rooms. *See* fitting rooms
dressmakers, 11–12
dry goods stores, 15

education, 89, 91–92. *See also* physical education
ethnic diversity, in bathing traditions, 39–40
exclusion: bathing and, 38–39, 42, 44, 46, 51, 62; comfort stations and, 76, 81–82; gender and, 6; key variables of, 6–7; privacy and, 2–3, 6, 112
exercise, 89. *See also* physical education

Farber, David, 118n22
Finnish immigrants, 39–40
fitting rooms, 5; bodies and, 9; class and, 6, 25–26, 34–35; emergence of, 16; in floor plans, 20; gender and, 22–25; human element with, 30–35; layout and design of, 9, 20–26, *21*; for men, 29; privacy and, 16, 20–26, 30–35; saleswomen and, 30–34, *31*. *See also* clothing; department stores

Fleischman Baths, 40–41, *41*
floor plans, for department stores, 16–17, 18–19, *19*
Florida, 1
Fraser Department Store, *21*, 21–22

gay men, 85–86, 117n21, 118n22
Gay New York (Chauncey), 117n21
gender, 1–2; bathing and, 39–40, 42; changing conceptions of, 114; class and, 6; comfort stations and, 63–64, 73–75; dressmaking and, 11–12; exclusion and, 6; fitting rooms and, 22–25; locker rooms and, 7, 99–100, 103–5, 109; physical education and, 100–105; privacy and, 3, 6–7, 19–20, 23–29, 52–53, 55, 99–100; private bathhouses and, 40–41, *41*; public baths and, 51–57, 60; public toileting and, 66–68; transgender individuals, 1–2. *See also* transgender individuals; women
Godey's Lady's Book, 11–13

health, public, 48–49, 82–83, 89, 92–93, 99
home: bathing in, 38–39, 42–46, *43, 45*; clothing and, 10–13; privacy and, 10–11, 117n19
hotel parlors, 118n22
hygiene, 37, 46–52, 58–60, 68, 83, 93, 99. *See also* bathing; cleanliness

immigrants, 6–7, 39–40, 50–51, 68, 91–92, 94, 98
industrial bathing, 41–42, *43*
industrialization, 7, 41, 44, 93, 100, 117n19
isolation, privacy and, 21–22, 44, 86

jersey waist, 14
Johnson, Arthur, 85

Leach, William, 15
locker rooms, 5–6; bathing and, 96–97; class and, 90–91, 110; cleanliness and, 94–95, 97–98, 110–11; gender and, 6–7, 99–100, 103–5, 109; opposition to, 95–96; physical education and, 94; privacy and, 90, 99–100,

110–11; socialization and, 90; surveillance in, 6, 90–91, 105–9. *See also* physical education

L. S. Ayers & Co., 27

Macy's, 18, 23–24
men: clothing for, 13; department store layouts and, 26; fitting rooms for, 29; gay, 85–86, 117n21, 118n22; in public baths, 55–57; public urination by, 66–67. *See also* gender
middle class. *See* class
modesty, 4–5, 60, 110

Norden, Bruce, 38, 55
North Carolina, 1

Oldenziel, Ruth, 117n20

Painesdale High School, 89, *90*, 93, 103, *104*, 105, *109*
pandemic, 114
Paul Revere School, 95, *106*
Penner, Barbara, 117n20
physical education, 129n2; arguments for, 93–94; class and, 94–95; emergence of, 89; gender and, 100–105; privacy and, 100–109, *101–4*, *106–9*; in public schools, 92–100, *96*. *See also* locker rooms
"pin-to-the-form" technique, 12
pregnancy, 28
privacy: bathing and, 38–39, 44–46; "bathroom bills" and, 1–2; bathrooms and, 44–46; bodies and, 37; class and, 3–5, 26, 90, 113, 117n21; comfort stations and, 63–64, 69–70, 72–73, 75–82; contestation of, 5–6; department stores and, 18; exclusion and, 2–3, 6, 112; fitting rooms and, 16, 20–26, 30–35; gender and, 3, 6–7, 19–20, 23–29, 52–53, 55, 99–100; home and, 10–11, 117n19; isolation and, 21–22, 44, 86; locker rooms and, 90, 99–100, 110–11; physical education and, 100–109, *101–4*, *106–9*; power and, 37; protection and, 3; public baths and, 51–53, 57–58; social construction of, 26–30, 112; as socially contested, 2–3, 112
Progressive movement, 7, 37, 91, 129n2

public baths. *See* baths, public
public health, 48–49, 82–83, 89, 92–93, 99
public schooling, 89, 91–92. *See also* locker rooms; physical education

racial segregation, 6, 78–82, *79*, 118n21
railroad cars, 117n20
restrooms, public, 5; legislation over transgender individuals and, 1–2; racial segregation in, 6; visual separation in, 118n22. *See also* comfort stations
Richter, Amy G., 117n20

Saaranen, Elnore, 39–40, 103–4, 110
saleswomen, in department stores, 30–34, *31*
saloons, toileting in, 65–66
Sandoval-Strausz, A. K., 117n20
schooling, 89, 91–92. *See also* locker rooms; physical education
segregation: gender, 19–20, 22, 24–30, 46, 53–57, 73–75, 99–105, 114; racial, 6, 78–82, *79*, 118n21
sewing, 10–11, 15
sexuality, 6, 85–86, 118n22
shirtwaist, 13–14
shopping, 15. *See also* department stores; fitting rooms
socialization, 2, 5–6, 90
socioeconomic status. *See* class
sound, in comfort stations, 72–73
Stoner, Eliza, 117n20, 118n22
stores. *See* department stores
Strawbridge & Clothier, *16–17*, 18, *19*, 26, 28, 31–32, 34
students. *See* children; locker rooms; physical education
surveillance: in locker rooms, 6, 90–91, 105–9; in public baths, 37, 42, 51, 60–62; in public restrooms, 86–87

taboo, 4
toileting, 65–68
toilets. *See* comfort stations; restrooms, public
train cars, 117n20
transgender individuals, 1–2
try-on rooms, 29. *See also* fitting rooms

upper class. *See* class
urbanization, 4, 7, 44, 68, 92–94, 100
urinals, 66–67, *67*, 71–72, *72*, 83
urination, public, 66–67. *See also* comfort stations; toileting
Utah, 1

Wanamaker's, 9, 18, 27, 29
Weismuller, Louis, 85
William Doerflinger Co., 23, *23*

women: comfort station use by, 74–75; as department store saleswomen, 30–34, *31*; department stores and, 18; dressmaking and, 11–12; pregnant, 28; in public baths, 54–56; public toileting by, 67–68; sewing and, 10–11. *See also* gender
working class. *See* class

youth. *See* children